i'm
so
glad
you're
here

i'm
so
glad
you're
here

a memoir

PAMELA GAY

SHE WRITES PRESS

Published 2020
Printed in the United States of America
ISBN: 978-1-63152-874-3
ISBN: 978-1-63152-875-0
Library of Congress Control Number: 2019920289

For information, address:
She Writes Press
1569 Solano Ave #546
Berkeley, CA 94707

Interior design by Tabitha Lahr

She Writes Press is a division of SparkPoint Studio, LLC.

For my beloved parents,
Helen Julia (Carr) and Charles Channing Gay,
and my children Raphael and Angela

contents

We never tell the story whole because a life isn't a story; it's a whole Milky Way of events and we are forever picking out constellations from it to fit who and where we are.

—Rebecca Solnit

I want to make clear from the start that I am telling this story. I am also part of the story, but the act of storytelling allows me to separate myself. I am seefin', as my mother said as a child. Seeing how things are, she explained to me—that's seefin'.

—Pamela Gay

A memoir proceeds perhaps more as memory does, in brief, episodic flashes illuminated by an overall picture of a central consciousness.

—Robin Hemley

PRELUDE

turkey day

I WAS EIGHTEEN and home from college on Thanksgiving break. It was my mother's birthday. John F. Kennedy had just been shot. And my father was being carried out on a stretcher.

"Don't-let-her-see, keep-her-away," I heard my two brothers shush as they lifted the stretcher.* I froze, as if by remaining still, they would not see me see him: his arms strapped to his side, his elbows locked; his body bound in a straitjacket, then sunk in a stretcher like a furrow in a field; his eyes, the only part of his body not restrained. They couldn't restrain his eyes: two black dots flickering in the light, darting wildly back and forth.

They carried him out the door and my mother followed, pausing in the doorframe. I watched her fling a kerchief over her head, tie a knot under her chin, then turn and ask me would-I-watch-the-turkey.

I nodded yes; I would watch the turkey, not TV.

A simple request, as if my mother were going on a quick run to the grocery store and would be right back, as if there would be a dinner, a feast, a celebration, as if the turkey would be eaten. But above her words, my mother's eyes stared blankly. She couldn't do a thing about it, none of it: Kennedy's death right on TV for all the world to see or her husband's breakdown for our eyes only.

I entered the doorframe and stood still as a still life, listening to the ambulance taking them away, no siren, the sound of tires rolling down the gravel driveway, fading into the distance.

I walked toward the muffled sound of the TV in the living room, turned the sound off, and watched images of Kennedy's body being carried into an ambulance played over and over as if no one could believe it.

The house fell silent except for an occasional hiss from the turkey roasting in the oven.

I sat on the gray kitchen linoleum, propped up against a cupboard next to the oven and waited.

I listened.

The turkey hissed and hissed.

When darkness fell suddenly like a curtain,

I tensed, lost in the dark,

frightened by the sizzling turkey sounding

closer and closer.

I must stay very still.

My breathing was too loud.

The doorbell rang, sending me into a state of alarm.

Who? Who? would come here now?

I hesitated, then decided I had better open the door. Perhaps it was important.

My friend Bob stood facing me. "What are you doing? I didn't think anyone was home. Your house is all dark, no car in the drive. Where *is* everyone?"

"Something came up. They had to go out," I said, keeping him in the doorframe.

"I just wanted to tell you that Tommy was coming for Christmas break."

I looked at him blankly. The turkey hissed.

"Tommy, the guy from Maine you spent all summer with." Instead of me, he didn't say.

"Oh, that's nice."

"Nice?"

I nodded blankly. "I've-gotta-go-watch-the-turkey," I blurted, easing the door toward him.

"Can I call you later?"

"Sure," I replied, shutting the door, leaving him in the dark.

I heard the porch door shut, then turned and walked across the small kitchen past the gateleg table and sat back down on the gray linoleum floor in front of the oven. I hugged my knees and listened to the turkey hissing, hissing in the dark, hot oven, fat dripping like sweat from its headless body. Memory of my mother sewing a flap of skin over its neck cavity to keep the stuffing in. This dead turkey this day, my only companion.

My mother had asked me to watch the turkey, but I couldn't see the turkey. I sat in the dark alone, so alone. There was no window for viewing. I opened the oven door and sat cross-legged, watching the turkey. Then I turned off the oven. After a while, the turkey stopped hissing.

I remembered the turkey I had colored in second grade, each feather a different color, all its feathers spread like a peacock. A happy turkey. Not a turkey beheaded for the oven. And then I grew sad, so sad: my father, my mother, JFK, and the turkey, Turkey Day.

*I remember my brothers were there. Decades later when talking to a sister-in-law, I learned that they were not there. "What? Are you sure?" I asked. "Absolutely," she said. I must have wished they were there to protect me. I wrote them into my memory.

FLASHBACK: MEMORY SLIDE

My father had planned to work until he was sixty-five, but his long-time employer forced him to retire at age sixty-two. He was devastated by this news. The depression that had been lurking throughout his life accelerated, and he experienced several psychotic episodes.

Age Seventeen: Memory of my father in our two-toned blue DeSoto, my mother driving, me in the back seat.

"They're coming after me!" my father shouted. "Hurry, hurry!" He turned toward my mother, then round to the rear window, his eyes wide, looking through me to somewhere beyond.

"Who? Who, Dad?" I shouted as I turned to look out the rear window, half expecting gangsters with guns.

"The IRS!" he screamed, opening the door to try to jump out.

Picture my mother: one hand on the steering wheel, her other hand reaching to pull the door shut, the car screeching to a halt on the roadside.

shock treatment

I WENT TO visit my father at Northampton State Hospital. I stood in the doorway of a bare, white-walled room and stared at my ghost of a father flat out in bed, his body tied down by some kind of physical restraint around his waist. His eyes, fixed in a permanent gaze, stared at the ceiling. I drew a deep, shuddering breath at the unspeakable sight of my father. I tried to say "Dad," again, "Dad," but the word wouldn't come out. Tears swelled inside but wouldn't release. I stood still, locked in the doorframe by an invisible emotional restraint, a transistor radio tucked under an arm.

A voice from behind: "You can't bring that in." I slowly turned my head. "No stim-u-la-tion allowed," a white-coated psychiatrist enunciated, to be sure I understood. I held the radio tight, lowering my eyelids, trying to process what was happening. I had no words. "I'll walk out with you," he said.

As we walked down the long, gray, tunnel-like corridor, we passed a dormitory style room crammed with beds. The psychiatrist told me that my father was being secluded because they were going to start shock treatments soon. Having your own room would normally be thought of as good unless it meant you'd be drugged and tied down so you couldn't escape, I didn't say. "A patient needs to be calm and quiet before this treatment," he said, pausing at the hospital entrance. My father didn't look "calm and quiet." I remembered how frightened he looked going out of our house in a straitjacket on a stretcher. Now he was "drugged out of his mind." Speechless, I walked under the red neon **EXIT** sign and out the door of the mental hospital, as if I could walk away and leave it all behind.

Later, sitting with my mother at the kitchen table, I asked her if—

She put her hand over my hand, assuring me that I would not lose my mind, that it wasn't contagious.

a change of scenery

MY FATHER HAD twenty-eight shock treatments. Thinking a change of scenery would do him good, my mother sold our house in western Massachusetts and moved with my father to Miami, where my sister lived, leaving me in a college dorm room across the river from where I grew up. I felt abandoned, left Standing on a Curb with the memory of "Turkey Day" stuck in my body and both my parents gone missing. The shock I experienced stayed buried. It would wait like the turkey in the oven.

My mother bought a trailer for temporary housing near my sister, who was living in Miami at the time. She tried keeping my father home. When I visited during spring break, I found him sitting in a chair outside the trailer and staring beyond where I was standing so I almost wanted to turn around and look. "I lived my life all wrong," he said to me when I was just coming of age. "I should have gone to Chicago, taken that offer. I was wrong," he repeated, looking right through me, it seemed, right through the clear blue Florida sky. Soon after, my mother had him admitted to a Florida state (psychiatric) hospital.

When I flew down to visit him, a member of the hospital staff brought him out to meet me. We sat at a table across from each other in an open atrium-like area. He asked me if I would like a Coke. I was surprised. I never liked soda, and I didn't remember him drinking soda, but I wanted to please him. "Sure," I said. He got up and brought two Cokes back for us—two *imaginary* Cokes. He set mine down in front of me, and I lifted my imaginary Coke to my lips. I don't remember what we talked about or if we even talked. I remember concentrating on sipping my Coke and his asking if I would like another. "No thank you," I said politely.

My mother could not bear to see my father wandering around as if in an alternative universe. The antipsychotic medication he was given, whether the dosage or the particular drug, was causing my father to hallucinate, which is what had sent him to a state mental hospital in the first place. She obtained permission for his release under her care with the understanding that he would see a psychiatrist.

And she made another decision. Medical expenses had nearly depleted my father's modest pension. I would need to quit going to college, she told me, standing in a telephone booth in a hallway in the dorm. I was the only one in the family to go to college. I wanted to pursue my education. I wouldn't quit, no I wouldn't. I was determined to expand my horizons. I obtained a local scholarship, worked twenty hours a week in a restaurant, overloaded courses, graduated in three years, married at age twenty, and set off on my new life, which could also be called "a change of scenery."

My husband enrolled in a PhD program at the University of Massachusetts in Amherst, and I took a job teaching English to high school students. Later I would take a graduate course called "The Dark Side of Robert Frost" and write about Frost's poem "Home Burial" without making any connection at the time to my "home burial." But the time would come.

DECADES LATER: 1995

Children are always episodes in someone else's narrative.
—Carolyn Steedman

standing on a curb

Galway City, Ireland
Fall 1995

STANDING ON A Curb in Galway City, saying good-bye at the end of an affair as my now former lover gets in his car, starts pulling out—I weep. Tears waterfall down my cheeks. He stops, gets out of the car, and holds me, hugs me. "Let's go back up to the room," he says, where we had spent the night, and I would spend another night before heading out to the Aran Islands in the morning.

"I don't know what came over me," I said as we sat up in bed, his arm around me.

"I thought this is what you wanted," he said, licking my tears.

"I do," I said, wiping away the last tear.

"In the past, I always saw you off first and then I left. You wanted to stay an extra week on your own, go to the Aran Islands. I have to go back to work. I asked if you were sure."

"I think I'm just tired. I'll stay here and rest."

"Sure?"

"Sure. Thanks for the hug. And licking my tears. I've never had anyone—"

15

"Shhh," he whispered as I curled up with myself and he gently tucked me in with a blanket for comfort. I closed my eyes. Then he drifted away.

That evening I went to a concert featuring traditional Irish music, everyone clapping, smiling, ending the night with song. It wasn't until much later that I realized that Standing on a Curb while someone I had been close to drove away triggered that feeling of abandonment that was stuck in my body. There were other "curbstone" endings, too, though no more on actual curbs, just the same feeling: loved and left, start-stop-blank (everything gone gray).

help

YOU'RE ALWAYS TRAVELING, my sister's voice echoed as I boarded a ferry off the west coast of Ireland where I'd spent the month of August. *What are you running away from? Why don't you stay home?* "Where you belong" was the implication. But I didn't feel as if I belonged. The house where I lived in Upstate New York wasn't home. It was where I stayed when I was working as a professor at a state university. I traveled whenever I could, most recently to Paris, Provence, Switzerland, and London at the invitation of a British philosopher with whom I had what he called "an international affair," which had ended in Ireland. Standing on deck, looking out to sea, my thoughts wandered like the mist that kept shifting, hovering as if trying to decide where to land.

A streak of blue cracked through the mist as the ferry landed and I headed to the airport to take a plane to New York City. I was looking forward to spending my fall sabbatical in the city where I had earned a PhD at New York University a decade earlier.

On the plane, I closed my eyes and traveled to Florida where my mother lurked like a shadow. I knew she was worn down from challenges she faced living with my father in the long aftermath of his "nervous breakdown" and now endless visits to the nursing home ten miles away. I planned to call her once I had settled and to see her over Thanksgiving. First, I needed to find a sublet. While temporarily staying with a friend on the Lower East Side, I received a call from my mother. She had taken to calling me on Sunday mornings and asking, "How's my baby girl?" It was Saturday morning, and I imagined she couldn't wait.

"I need your help," my mother said quietly, desperation in her voice.

"Right now? I've just arrived."

"Your father cries every time they bring him food," she said as if she hadn't heard me. "He's such a dignified man. I didn't want them to do it."

"Do what?" I asked, confused and a little scared.

"Insert a feeding tube. They-had-to-restrain-him," my mother said, running the words together as if that were the only way she could get them out.

"Wait, but I thought he signed a paper that said he didn't want—"

"He signed the wrong line on the form," my mother said.

Since at the time he couldn't remember how old he was, what state he lived in, what season it was, then how would he know what he was signing? I wanted to ask. Instead I asked if she could make the change, "given the circumstances" is how I put it.

She told me that she worried if she changed what he signed, "someone" in the family would accuse her of murder. By "someone" I understood she meant my older sister.

"Have you talked to Cynthia?" I asked.

My mother skirted the question and told me that my sister and her husband Jim would stop and visit in November when they drove from Long Island to Miami to try to reconnect with some old business contacts.

"They can't stay," my mother said.

"You mean you want *me* to stay?" I asked to be sure I understood. I didn't ask about my older brothers Doug and Jerry, who rarely called her.

"Look, I know you have work to do, but you can work here," my mother said. "You can stay in the guest bedroom. I can clear out a couple of drawers and make some room in the closet, and we can bring in a table from the porch," my mother went on, a burst of excitement in her voice. "I'll pay for your plane ticket," she added, as if trying to entice me with bonus points. "I need your help," my mother, who never asked for help, said again. "No one else can come." Her voice faded until it came to a full stop.

After my father's nervous breakdown and the move to Florida, I was only able to visit once or twice a year. I was struggling in the aftermath of a divorce and trying to raise two children while working and pursuing a PhD. I began thinking that this would be a good opportunity to reconnect with my mother. We'd have some time together—just the two of us. And sublets in Manhattan were quite expensive, I had discovered, not surprisingly, from my brief perusal of ads in the *Village Voice*. I could also get a lot of work done. There wasn't much to do at Sun Ray Homes except catch some sunrays in the backyard and drink fresh orange juice. I was also glad, proud even, that I was now in a position to help. I was tenured, my daughter was in college, my son in graduate school—and I could pay for the plane ticket.

"Yes, I'll come. Of course, I'll come. Help's on its way."

"I'm so glad," my mother said, her voice trailing off like a sigh of relief.

welcome to sun ray homes

TEN DAYS LATER I flew into Orlando and took an hour-long taxi ride south to Frostproof. Originally called Keystone City, it had been renamed Frostproof after surviving the Great Freeze of 1895 when temperatures dropped into the teens along the Ridge that runs one hundred miles from Leesburg to Sebring, virtually wiping out the Florida citrus industry. Legend has it that people from all over the Ridge came to marvel at this Garden of Eden in the middle of the new wasteland. One hundred years later, the economy is still citrus-driven, though frost has killed the citrus from time to time. But the name holds and is used as a marketing ploy to attract potential homebuyers and some tourists who might be inclined to stop and buy some "frostproof" oranges on their way to somewhere else.

As my parents grew older, they became tired of the increased congestion in the Fort Lauderdale area. Picture my father sitting in his chair in the living room of their attached two-bedroom home in Cooper City looking at ads in a newspaper. He sees an ad for a new housing development on the edge of Frostproof in central Florida and is keen on moving there. It will be quiet, and in his mind, a good deal. My mother will later regret their decision to move there. My mother is not keen on leaving, but she goes along with it, a decision she later regrets.

Shortly after the taxi turned onto Highway 27, I spotted a sign for Ridge Island Groves in Haines City, the heart of the citrus industry, and asked the driver to stop. I bought a bag of red navel oranges. "Cara Cara," the salesperson said, explaining that they'd been discovered at the Hacienda de Cara Cara in Valencia, Venezuela and brought to Florida where they've done well.

On one of my visits before my father could no longer drive, he took me for a ride on some back roads through a nearby grove: endless rows of trees with dark green leaves lined up like very tall boxwood hedges bearing oranges. I asked him to stop so I could take a photo that would go beautifully with Benjamin Rosenbaum's short-short story "The Orange" that I often read with my students. (I still have the photo of a ripe orange hanging on a branch, ready to fall or be picked.) The story concerns an orange who humbly accepted the honor of ruling the world from a simple branch in a grove in Florida and how everyone wept with joy and the governor of Florida declared every day a holiday.

But when the orange said, "It is time," no one would pick it. An outsider from Chicago had to be brought in. I was an outsider who had been brought in to pronounce, "It is time," time for my father to take leave at the ripe old age of ninety-three.

Ours was a sundered family. I felt more like an observer than a participant. Growing up, what I knew about my siblings was mostly based on what I saw Standing in the Hallway of our modest, ivory-colored Cape Cod style house.

My brother Doug was ten years older than me. I must have been five or six when I saw him reach for a slab of hardened fudge frosting off the Depression-era "wacky" cake our mother had made and stored on top of the refrigerator. "Who did that?" she teasingly asked when she went to serve the cake after dinner. I think she knew and must have been pleased that her cooking gave such pleasure. How I enjoyed that it was our secret. In 1955, when

Doug was twenty, he looked like James Dean in *Rebel Without a Cause*: his coal black hair slicked back, his eyebrows thick, wearing an unbuttoned shirt with the collar turned up over a white T-shirt and jeans. He left home and married soon after he graduated from high school. I never saw much of him after that.

While my brother Jerry was closer to me in age (six years older), his mental health problems made any kind of relationship with him challenging. Late one afternoon, when I was five or six, our mother asked Jerry to keep an eye on me while she walked to the corner store to pick up something for dinner. After she left, all the lights went out. *Where is my brother?* I tiptoed through the hallway to make my way to the porch door, thinking he must be outside. I had to go through the kitchen first. Just as I started to go around the wringer washing machine, he popped up from behind and shouted, "Boo!" Then he went out the door, leaving me in the dark. When I went into the backyard to look for him, he eyed me with a malicious-looking smile that frightened me. He turned around and opened the pen where he kept a collie dog he'd been given as payment for working for a breeder one summer, put him on a leash, and walked away without looking at me or saying a word. Feeling abandoned and scared, I sat down on the grass and cried so loud that a neighbor heard me, came over, and took me into her house, where she gave me a piece of just-baked blueberry pie.

After quitting high school, Jerry worked at a garage. On weekends, he'd fix up cars in our driveway to sell; he could take an engine apart and put it back together. Standing in the Hallway one evening, I heard some kind of disturbance in the kitchen and saw my mother talking to a cop. He told her that Jerry had gotten into a car in our driveway and driven fast across our yard, bashing the whole side of a neighbor's garage. My mother handled the problem, which required immediate payment and no doubt some juggling of her modest budget. Turning my head to the left, I would have seen our father in his chair in the living room.

He never wanted to get involved and left any conflict up to our mother to handle, which she did in the kitchen.

When I was in junior high, I brought a friend home with me after school. As we headed for the porch door, we both eyed a case of beer under the maple tree by the entrance. I shrugged my shoulders as if I couldn't begin to explain. I wondered what we would find when we went inside and whether I would be embarrassed or perhaps scared. My mother, who was at work, wouldn't be home for a couple of hours. She'd left me a note to put some potatoes in the oven. We found Jerry in the living room, his collar turned up on his pink pinwale corduroy shirt, sitting in our father's recliner drinking beer and watching an old western on our black-and-white TV, with his feet up on the hassock. We both eyed him and went upstairs to what was now my room. I forgot to put the potatoes in the oven.

Occasionally, Jerry would slip me a five-dollar bill.

Doug and Jerry were not close but they sometimes got into mischief together. Standing in the Hallway when both my brothers were home, I saw a cop appear at the door, this time about a complaint made by the owners of Wilson's Rest Home down the street. My brothers apparently had been taking turns climbing a ladder so they could peer into the windows and make grotesque faces and sounds to scare the residents.

While my sister was twelve years older, and I was nine when she left home to get married, I have more memories of her than of my brothers. It must have been hard for her when I arrived. There were only two bedrooms for children upstairs: the boys' room and the girls' room. At age twelve, I don't imagine she wanted to share her room with a baby. I was put in a crib in the dining room and later moved to a cot in my sister's room where she was less and less present.

What I knew about my siblings as adults was mostly based on what my mother told me. They seemed more like distant cousins, as if we had been raised in different families and didn't have the same mother. My brothers stayed in Massachusetts near where they grew up, though they didn't see much of each other, and I didn't see much of either of them. Their occasional visits to our parents in Florida were more of a stop on the way to vacationing somewhere else. My sister and her husband visited more often, especially as our parents grew older. And several times, they took them on vacation—Lauderdale-by-the-Sea, Sanibel Island—or flew them to Long Island where Cynthia and Jim were living. On one visit, they drove our parents back to Vermont where they had both grown up, my father in Brattleboro, my mother in Brandon.

I tried to remember when we were last all together. Maybe at our parents' fiftieth wedding anniversary that my sister had arranged in Florida? But were my brothers there? Soon we would all be together for our father's funeral.

I glanced out the window again and saw the sign for Frostproof. A few miles and some orange groves later, the familiar billboard came into view: WELCOME TO SUN RAY HOMES. The sign featured a drawing that might have been used in a proposal for this housing development "where some of the nicest people live." The sign featured a drawing that might have been used in a proposal for this housing development. To the left, the top of a palm tree leaned over some charcoal-colored lines meant to be sunrays. A simple drawing of a basic concrete block house looked like mass-produced post-World War II housing, functional and economical. In the space below the billboard, raised up by several two-by-fours, I could see some of the houses on streets crisscrossing this flatland. Above the billboard in full color was the ever-present blue sky.

Next to the entrance was a funeral parlor with a hearse parked out front "at the ready," though I don't imagine that was part of the plan. The streets all had men's names—Thomas, Walter, Charles, Raymond. The taxi turned onto Stanley. My father's name was Charles. "Couldn't you find a house on Charles?" I asked my mother.

When the taxi pulled into the driveway, I saw my mother peering through the sheer curtains in the picture window. I put my suitcase down and walked up the pathway to the pink stucco house, my arms around a bag of oranges, and stood on the pink flamingo welcome mat. Then a click in the lock and the front door opened. "I'm so glad you're here," my mother said, hugging me, the bag of oranges squeezed between us. I set the bag down and went to pick up my suitcase. Coming up the walkway again, I gazed at my mother smiling in the pink-framed doorway and noticed how much older she looked. She was on the brink of her eighty-sixth birthday; I was almost fifty. I stepped into the frame and we hugged again, my arms around her shoulders, hers around my waist.

"I see the books I sent ahead have arrived," I said, walking around the pile of boxes in the hallway outside the guest bedroom. The twin beds were covered with white cotton chenille bedspreads from the 1950s, dotted with rows of raised white dots that looked like tiny pom-poms. I put my suitcase down on the oval New England braided rug my mother had placed over the glossy, marble-speckled terrazzo floor. When my mother couldn't sleep, she sometimes rested on one of the twin beds and watched a late night program on a small, portable TV on top of a bureau where she kept assorted spools of thread, needles, embroidery hoops, googly eyes to glue on dolls she made, and leftover scraps of cloth.

When I returned to the living room, my mother complimented me on my Louise Brooks bob, circa 1920: geometric, sharp, my hair colored dark. "You had a nice-looking bob I recall from a photo," I said, noticing that her short perm-curled, salt-and-pepper hair had grown whiter since I'd seen her last.

"Yes, parted on the side with rows of waves," she said, perking up. "Are you hungry?" She headed into the dining room just as the cuckoo clock cuckooed five times.

"I'm starved," I said, knowing this was her dinner hour and she had been waiting all afternoon for me to join her.

"I know you're a vegetarian now," she said, going into the kitchen and opening a cupboard door. "Your sister said since you'll be here awhile I'd better stock up on cans of beans," she said proudly, pointing to the display. Tonight she'd made broccoli soup, corn fritters, and salad. She motioned me to sit down at the end of the table where my father used to sit.

"Your corn fritters are delicious," I said. "He so enjoyed your cooking." We continued in silence. I thought about how my father always took his time eating, carefully cutting everything on his plate and chewing slowly. It wasn't a conscious act to aid digestion. And he wasn't following the Buddhist practice of mindful eating. It was just his way.

"Apple pie?" my mother asked.

I remembered my father liked apple pie warm, topped with a slice of Vermont cheddar cheese.

As we ate our dessert, my mother told the story of the time my father tried to escape from the nursing home. "They found him in someone's car in the parking lot," my mother said. "They don't know how he got out." We laughed, for a moment admiring his ingenuity.

"I've known him since I was nineteen," my mother whispered, pointing to a framed sepia-toned photo of the two of them before they were married. "And now he won't speak to me. He won't even look at me."

I walked over to my mother and put my arm around her. "He wants out. It's time," I said, pulling up a chair next to her.

"He was such a dignified man," she said.

"Let's not take that away from him now." She nodded in agreement.

Later in the evening after my mother went to bed, I sat in my father's recliner in the living room and studied that photo. My mother's head is propped against his shoulder. One arm is nestled around his waist; the other rests on her waist, her fingers folded in a fist, as if holding onto the excitement her eyes and shy smile reveal.

My father—tall, handsome, and fashionably dressed in a starched white shirt, striped tie, gray suit jacket with Gatsby-esque lapels, and white trousers and shoes—gazes into the eye of the camera, his head slightly tilted. Both have dark hair parted on the left side—his hair smooth, straight, razor-edge sharp, perfectly completing his oval-shaped face; her hair, loosely finger-waved in a bob, softening her round face. She is wearing a lightly colored, long-sleeved, criss-crossed jersey and matching below-the-knee skirt. In a few months, the stock market will crash but they don't know that yet.

My mother is completing her studies at a business institute where she has just won first place in a shorthand contest. My father is a manager of the tool department in a hardware store where he will work for forty years. He will become well known in the hardware business, even featured in an ad in *Hardware Age,* a leading trade magazine in the 1950s.

But the sepia-toned photo is a *before* photo: before they married and began a family, before the Great Depression, and before my father's great depression that, unknown to my mother at the time of their marriage, was lurking. For a moment, I imagined myself intervening in my parents' relationship, warning them off. "Stop! Don't do it," I say to them, coupled together in the sunlight, her smile innocent, eager, his handsome face camera-ready, and oh, those stylish white trousers and shoes.

I put my feet up on the burgundy faux-leather hassock and stared at the blank TV screen, thinking about my father, my mother, aging, and the next morning when I would go to help my father. My mother was not the only parent who needed help. I rose and closed the heavy gold drapes over the sheer curtains in the picture window, as my father had done every night when he lived here in this home, where now the sun's rays have faded into sunset time.

it's time

THE NEXT MORNING, my mother and I sat out on the back porch for breakfast: fresh orange juice, coffee, and cinnamon buns.

"I remember how much you loved my cinnamon buns," my mother said.

"I remember when all the neighborhood children used to line up outside the porch door for a slice of your just-baked bread," I said.

My earliest memories of my mother are her baking and sewing and working in her flower garden. She stayed at home until I was eleven. Then she learned to drive and went to work as a bookkeeper.

"I'd better get going," I said, getting up from my chair. I assured her that I wouldn't do anything without her approval. She looked relieved. I suggested she rest on the chaise lounge on the porch. "We'll talk when I get back. I won't be long," I said, handing her the local newspaper she liked to read in the morning. After I went back into the kitchen to bring in the dishes and fetch her car keys, I looked at her through the window over the sink. Her eyes were closed. One hand rested on the newspaper on her lap.

On the ten-mile drive to the nursing home, I thought about the last time I saw my father when I visited in April. It was lunchtime. He was sitting in a chair in the corridor waiting to go to the dining room. My mother had to point him out. I would not have recognized him. He was wearing a baseball cap and a pink alligator polo shirt with the collar turned up. My mother told me that my sister and her husband had given him the cap and shirt and that he wore the cap every day when he sat in the hallway "to see what's going on." When he worked, he always wore starched white shirts; when he retired, he still wore button-down shirts, but they were cotton and pastel-colored with short sleeves. He never wore pink. He did have a hat rack with hats for different occasions, gardening, etc., but never a baseball cap.

He broke into a grin upon seeing me, then rose, grabbing a side rail as he struggled to walk down the corridor without help, his shoes clicking with each step.

At lunch I cut up his food and handed him a fork. He headed straight for the lemon meringue pie. A nurse told me he wasn't eating much. I suggested she bring the dessert after.

My mother's social life at the time revolved around residents, as they were called, in the nursing home. She greeted everyone. "You have to meet Leo," she said when a very thin man was wheeled in. "He doesn't eat," she whispered, and pointed to his untouched tray of food. "And that woman," my mother explained, pointing across the table to a gray-haired woman who was trying to feed a doll carrots mixed with lemon meringue pie, "is sitting in your father's place."

After guiding my father back to his room to rest and we were heading out the front door, my mother stopped for a moment. Then she turned to me and said, "She's gone." She was referring to another woman whom she was accustomed to seeing sitting by the door like a Walmart greeter, but holding on to a big beige pocketbook like my mother's, as if she were on her way out. I thought about how worn down my mother looked now, six months later, from going back and forth to the nursing home: having a look, then going back again to have another look at her husband—my father—dying, all the residents dying.

At the entrance now, I tapped the secret code and let myself in. No one greeted me. I went to the front desk to ask to see my father and to speak with the head nurse. Pausing in the doorway, I glimpsed my father flat out in bed, shrouded in white. Only his head showed. His eyes were closed. When I stood at his bedside, he didn't look up. I leaned in close and could hear him breathing. He didn't seem asleep. He seemed to be shutting down.

The head nurse appeared and suggested we talk outside the room in case he could hear us. I asked her about the use of a feeding tube when he was dying. She said that surgically implanting feeding tubes in elderly demented patients was routine, but when they tried to insert a tube into my father's stomach, he screamed so loud he terrorized the residents. They had to restrain him. "We tied his wrists down so he wouldn't pull the tube out again," she said.

My hands trembled. I was shocked seeing him like this. "I'm sure he doesn't want a feeding tube," I stuttered. "He signed the wrong line on the form. My mother didn't know what to do," I went on, emotionally distraught, trying to make a case. "And what about dying with dignity?" I pleaded.

When I saw that the head nurse was not moved, I got practical. "Legally, how do I go about reversing the decision as soon as possible?" I asked, and it turned out to be simple. I could bring back a form signed by my mother. I lingered at the door to my father's room. Another nurse stopped to ask me if she could be of help.

"What do you think about his being fed by a feeding tube?" I asked.

"I'm not allowed to say," she said. Then she took me to a room down the hall to see a woman with her eyes closed, her white hair pulled back gently in a bun, and her body buried in a mound of stiff white sheets. "Ten years like this," she said, "and her relatives have all gone, and now she's a ward of the state." On my way out, I stopped at the desk and picked up a form for my mother to sign.

On the drive back, I thought about my father's scream in protest and was so struck by a connection I made that I pulled over to the side of the highway. I was certain that being restrained again had triggered a horrific memory of his being restrained in a straitjacket before having electroshock treatments. His body remembered. He was re-traumatized. My body remembered, too. I drove fast down the highway as if this were an emergency, got my mother to sign the form to remove the feeding tube, and drove back to the nursing home. He would not die restrained.

meat vs. vegetables

MY MOTHER AND I hadn't lived together since I was seventeen, and my food tastes had completely changed. I was a vegetarian now and while my mother had said that wouldn't be a problem, that she ate lots of vegetables and she could always cook some meat for herself, dinner soon became a challenge.

She wasn't against vegetarianism in principle but she loved to cook, and what could she cook for me now? I did on occasion eat fish, but my mother preferred beef or chicken. A few weeks into my stay, I began preparing some dishes I missed: red beans and rice with steamed bok choy, spicy green curry noodles with snow peas. After all, I reasoned, my mother cooked steak. And so why shouldn't I marinate tofu? While she developed a greater understanding of vegetarian cuisine, she found this difference alienating.

The trouble began one evening when my mother started oohing and aahing about a juicy sirloin steak she had cooked. She loved her steak rare and said so but perversely, it seemed to me, went on talking about meat. I let it go the first time. Then my mother began cooking more and more meat and talking about her love of meat. And instead of cooking her steak outside on the grill, she began cooking it inside without turning on the exhaust fan. I never remembered my mother eating so much steak before. Finally, I asked her, kindly I thought, to put the kitchen fan on when she cooked or else use the grill outside. The smell was bothering me. "It's like smoking," I tried to explain. "If you don't smoke and someone comes over and smokes in your house, you can feel ill." My mother eyed me defiantly, as if she were a child being scolded for bad manners. Then she picked up her plate and took her meal out on the porch, where she had set up a TV tray next to her lounge chair, leaving me in the kitchen with the smell of steak.

I was frustrated and even angry with my mother, but when I looked out the window over the kitchen sink and saw her eating her meal alone, I felt compassion. It seemed to me that she was trying to hang onto something, something familiar, a habit, a way of being, and that her behavior was her way of expressing what she couldn't say. I couldn't eat. I looked at my plate of food—stir-fried blackened tofu with garlic-ginger-soy-honey sauce and vegetables over a bed of raw spinach and rice—and felt childishly selfish.

I wished, oh how I wished, I could call my sister and tell her we'd had a fight over meat vs. vegetables, and we'd laugh and talk about what to do. *What should we do, Cynthia?* I even dialed her number but hung up after a couple of rings, fearing she would be angry and shout at me. She always seemed antagonistic. I was on my own here and my mother wasn't so glad any more.

voila!

DURING MY STAY, my mother made a game of having my coffee ready the moment I appeared and said "Good morning." In her best high school French, she would reply "Bonjour," followed by "Voila," and there would be my Mocha Java in the French press I had brought with me. All I had to do was plunge and pour. I thought my mother had become childishly silly, but I had gotten used to the routine and even looked forward to her "rise and shine" greeting. I suspected, however, that underneath ran an undercurrent of judgment, as if to say, "So you think you are so sophisticated with your French press," which of course she would never say out loud.

But this morning there was no "Bonjour," no "Voila." My mother was sitting at the dining room table with her coffee and the newspaper. I was surprised to see her all dressed up in a pink-flowered blouse and pastel pink polyester pants that matched the color of the pink stucco house.

"It's almost time to go," I said, looking at the clock. "The nurse said we should come around 10:00, after they made the rounds."

"I'm not going this morning," she said. "Someone needs to be here when Cynthia and Jim arrive."

The night before, my sister had called to say that she and Jim were in Miami on business and would like to stop by before they continued to St. Pete and take her to lunch. When I answered the phone, I didn't greet her, didn't pause to say a few words even. "I'll get Mom," I blurted, handing the phone to our mother. I couldn't talk to her. She was trouble, my sister.

"We'll go to the nursing home after lunch," my mother said.

"Did you tell her they took out the feeding tube?" I asked, walking toward her, cup of java in hand. "He might not last the day."

"Chicken breasts are on sale at Publix. Maybe I should stop there today," she said, disappearing behind the newspaper. "Looks like it's going to be a nice day." She picked up her cup of instant Maxwell House coffee. "Good to the last drop," she added with a smile.

I walked back to the kitchen, hurriedly finishing my coffee. As I was washing the mug in the sink, I noticed that her special violet-patterned bone china teacup was turned upside down in the drainer. At the end of the counter, I saw a half-empty bottle of vodka.

It felt as if I'd walked into the wrong house. This wasn't my mother. My mother only used this teacup on special occasions. Her sister Madge had given her one teacup each year on her birthday. Sometimes when I visited, she'd suggest we have tea in the afternoon. "Tea for two," she'd say, removing two teacups from the cabinet, always choosing for herself the violet-patterned cup.

I recalled that Jim stored a couple of bottles of vodka in my mother's bedroom closet for when he and my sister visited, because there was no liquor in the house. He liked to have a vodka and tonic in the evening. The only time I could remember my mother having a drink was on Christmas Eve, when she'd have a glass of port wine and giggle like a girl.

I walked past my mother and opened the front door. I paused and turned around. Her head was buried in the newspaper again. She would have to wait.

going downhill

ON THE DRIVE to the nursing home, I glanced over at Publix and pictured my mother heading for the sale on chicken breasts. She'd be carrying her oversized, beige, faux leather pocketbook, which she took with her everywhere. It had several zipper compartments with business envelopes marked for groceries, gas, doctor, pharmacy, hair dresser, etc., each stuffed with cash.

A beep came from the car behind. I hadn't been paying attention. The red light had changed to green.

I pulled into Hillside and parked where my mother always parked. There were no hillsides in central Florida. Maybe the name for the nursing home was metaphorical for going downhill. I pressed the code to let myself in.

After the feeding tube was removed, my father began fading into the distance like a ship heading out to sea that in a short time would disappear from view. His kidneys were failing, but the diagnosis didn't matter. His body was beyond repair. *He's dying*, no one dared say. Now he was in a private room next door to the woman being kept alive by a feeding tube.

I pulled up a chair to sit with him. He didn't open his eyes. His lips were relaxed; his scream was gone. I closed my eyes and listened to him breathe. Then I studied his face: his carefully combed white hair and mustache and smooth olive skin. *He's still handsome*, I thought. His eyes flicked open for a moment, as if he had heard my thought.

Sitting alone now with my father as his body continued to shut down, I wanted to tell him I loved him. I wanted to story him with some loving memories and comfort my grieving self.

I am five. We are sitting together on the living room couch, and you are reading to me my favorite book—*Bunny Blue*, who lost and found his beautiful pink satin bow. What draws my attention is the secret nightlife of the toys in the toy chest. I identify with them, cheer them on. You must sense my enjoyment, for when I ask you to read the story again, you don't refuse. You don't say, "Again?" You don't say, "It's dinner time now." You don't say anything. You just read it again.

I am six. When you see me standing at the edge of your vegetable garden watching you hoe weeds, you stop and ask me if I would like a garden.

"Yes," I say.

"What shape?" you ask, putting your hoe down and walking toward me.

"A heart," I say, the first shape that comes to mind.

You smile and go into the garden shed and return with some clothesline and a spade. You outline a heart with the rope and edge the shape and divide the inside into neat squares. After you work hard shaking the soil loose and wipe the sweat from your forehead with a white pocket handkerchief, you ask me, "What color flowers would you like?"

"Red, orange, yellow, purple," I say.

"Ah, the colors of a rainbow, good colors for a butterfly garden," you say.

Around the edge, you plant red zinnias from my mother's flower garden and inside you sprinkle seeds that will become petunias, marigolds, purple aster, and black-eyed Susans. You are pushing me on a tree swing you made for me at the edge of the woods that bordered our acre of land.

"Higher," I say. "More." I want to go closer, ever closer to the blue sky. I want more swing time with you behind me: the scent of cherry tobacco from your pipe; soaring through the air but knowing you are there.

"Sundaes on Sunday," you joke, and off we go to Friendly's. I love the hot fudge sauce that slides down the snow-white vanilla bank, and our time together. We don't talk much. We sit quietly enjoying our treat. Then, "Ready?" you say. And we go the mile back home into a disquieting silence that feels like something unspoken is lurking.

I looked at my father now, flat out on an institutional bed, his eyes closed to life on the outside. How I wished he could hear me. I wanted to talk to someone. There was no one to listen, no one to hug my grieving self. I reached in my purse for a pen and something to write on. Sitting with my father dying, I looked down at the soft brown hue of a paper napkin, the color of leaves before they decompose. I picked up my pen and wrote:

I write to keep from crying. I am alone. I am at my father's side. I am filled with tears. He is breathing hard. He is wild with death. His mouth open, his teeth rotten. He is in pain. He struggles. He stares at me as out of a skeleton closet. He makes cries. His hands go up and down. How can a man so dignified die so undignified? He is scared, my father. He looks like a child's nightmare of a scarecrow. I am alone with him. I am upset with my mother, for she would not come, as she awaits my sister's arrival. My sister won't be here until much later, and my mother won't leave a key or a note—she says they've come a long way to see her. I wonder how she cannot sit with my father. She is the only one he responds to now, and why would he want to die alone? I do not understand. I can't bear that now and so I speak to this page. Should I ask for the feeding tube? Did I do right? He will get feverish now. My mother's behavior is strange—that she would just leave him, go to lunch. Where are the doctors? I feel like throwing up. A nurse comes and touches my shoulder. Tears flood at the human touch. How can I leave him? He doesn't see me truly—he doesn't want to be seen like this.

I reached for his hand, skeletal now like his garden fork, and began humming, not a tune, but a repeated low sound like a fog horn sending out a warning signal, allowing my emotions to run through me, sweep over and over like waves coming to shore, keening as if he were already gone.

As if he heard me, he winced and emitted a slight groan from pain making its way through his body. With his eyes still closed, he straightened his blanket, pulled it up, folded it back. Even while dying, he was trying to preserve his dignity. I got up to see about giving him some painkillers. A nurse told me they had nothing stronger than Tylenol. They'd have to get a doctor. It could be a while.

I mashed two Tylenol in some applesauce as my mother used to do when I was a child and had trouble swallowing pills.

I managed to get some down his throat. I sat with him until he fell asleep.

Where is my mother? Maybe she felt they had said good-bye yesterday. I replayed the scene I'd witnessed Standing in the Doorway. My father, conscious of his impending death, looked up at my mother and reached out to her with his hand. I was so moved I almost went toward him myself, but he only had eyes for her. My mother stood still for what seemed like a long moment, as if someone had hit the pause button for this scene. I watched my father close his eyes and my mother turn around, her golden hazel eyes glazed over, fixed in a faraway stare as she went out the door, brushing past me as if I weren't there.

I wanted to rewrite the scene with violins playing in a sentimental, black and white, old-fashioned movie, the kind my mother liked. Or, better yet, the song "I Only Have Eyes for You" crooned by Frank Sinatra with the Count Basie orchestra in 1962, the year I graduated from high school, though it's the 1959 version by the Flamingos that I remembered listening to in ninth grade, slow dancing bear hug style with a boy named Stanley in the tennis court outside the high school. In 1934, two years after my parents were married, my mother would have heard the original version sung by Dick Powell with Ruby Keeler in the musical *Dames*. But I couldn't imagine them dancing in the moonlight.

Six months into the marriage, my mother realized that she had made a mistake. She was already pregnant with my sister. The fun-loving man she thought she had married had a dark side that increasingly shadowed their relationship and eventually overshadowed him. My mother told me that she always wondered why the woman to whom my father had been engaged suddenly broke the engagement right before the wedding. "They had even bought furniture," she said. My mother suspected that the woman had known what my mother found out too late—that mental illness was rampant in my father's family.

My mother wanted out of the marriage long before I was born. My sister told me that when she was eleven our mother had told her she wanted to leave our father. "What do you think?" she'd asked.

"Imagine asking a child that," my sister said.

When my mother learned she was pregnant with a fourth child, she felt she couldn't leave, just as she must have felt when she was pregnant with my sister early in her marriage. She used to say of any difficulty, "This too shall pass," but this dark cloud would not pass until my father passed. Maybe as my father lovingly reached out to her on his deathbed, she felt it was too late.

Where is everyone? I shivered as I rose from the bedside chair and stood next to my father, his eyes shut. I leaned over and gently pressed my lips on his forehead as if to mark my presence. Then I went out of the room to call my mother.

"Your sister wants me to ask you something," my mother said. "She wants to know would we like to go to St. Pete, spend the night. Jim has to go there on business. She thinks it would do us good. We need a break."

"But he's dying. He won't last long."

"We'll stop and see him after lunch. They'll call if anything happens," she said.

Like death? I wondered. I told my mother I couldn't go, that I was going to stay a little while longer, then go back to her house and return later to be with him.

They hadn't invited me to lunch, but I wouldn't have gone anyway. I was upset about my mother's decision not to go with me that morning to the nursing home when my father was so close to death. Instead, she had chosen to wait for my sister and her husband to take her to lunch. I decided to go to a nearby public library where I sometimes worked on my writing and then head back to my mother's house, when I was sure they were gone.

suspicion

I WAS SURPRISED to see my mother when I opened the door to her house.

"I decided that I'd better not go to St. Pete," she said, limping from the dining room to the living room.

"Why are you limping?" I asked.

"Oh, it's my arthritis."

"Your ankle's swollen."

"Yes, it does that sometimes," she said, sitting down in her chair.

I looked at her suspiciously.

"Actually, I tripped and fell."

"I thought so. I think you should soak that ankle," I said, leaving to find a bucket and Epsom salt I remembered seeing. I knelt down by the bathtub and turned the water on to test the temperature, then added the salt. As the bucket was filling, I thought about my father dying, dying alone, whether he knew he was alone. A line from Robert Frost's poem "Home Burial" echoed: " . . . from the time when one is sick to death / One is alone, and he dies more alone."

The water spilled over like my thoughts. I turned the water off, then sat on the aqua bathmat on the edge of the tub and thought about my mother: her ankle, the china cup, the vodka bottle. One thing was clear—she certainly couldn't go back and see him now. But how could I leave her with one foot in a bucket? Maybe my mother would kick the bucket? *Not* funny, I reprimanded myself.

While my mother soaked her ankle, she told me about their visit to my father after lunch. "He wasn't any better," she said.

"Better?" I asked, sitting down on the crewel-embroidered footstool.

"And he didn't seem to know we were there. But before we left, he opened his eyes, and his eyes went so bright when he saw Jim."

I turned my head and looked out the picture window.

"He always liked Jim," my mother said. "He was like a son. Whenever he visited, he'd ask, 'What do you need done around here, Charlie?' He installed sprinklers in the lawn. They came on automatically so your father wouldn't have to wrestle with the hose. He always asked your father about his garden."

My thoughts wandered to my father's garden in the backyard of my childhood home—rows of vegetables, a line of cherry trees— and how behind this house he had created a smaller garden that looked like Mr. McGregor's garden in Beatrix Potter's book *The Tale of Peter Rabbit* that my father used to read to me.

"And he bought him that white hat."

The sun had already gone over the horizon. The crepuscular glow of the dimming light lingered. Darkness was about to fall. It was twilight time.

"Remember?"

I remembered a photo of him standing in front of an orange tree, smiling proudly, wearing an expensive, wide-brimmed white hat with a black band, a white suit, and white shoes. "Yes, yes, a Stetson, wasn't it?"

"Cost a hundred dollars. He looked like a rancher in that hat," she said, looking across the room at the blank TV screen as if tuning in a photo of him.

I glanced at my watch. "He won't last the night," I said, getting up from the footstool.

"Maybe there's something on TV," she said, as if she hadn't heard me.

I turned the TV on, handed her the program guide, and then went into the kitchen to get the car keys. As I headed for the front door, my mother threw the guide on the floor and declared there was nothing good on. What she wanted was to watch a movie, one of the old ones.

"A movie? You want me to get you a movie? *Now?*"

"Yes," she said, perking up a little, having got my full attention.

I'd have to drive ten miles to Blockbuster, just past the nursing home, then back to my mother's house and back out again. I wouldn't get to the home until after eight. I couldn't leave my mother unoccupied. "Here, watch *Jeopardy* until I return," I said, tuning in the show.

On the drive, I thought about how I had just acted toward my mother—like a parent with a sudden emergency might act with a child: "Sit here. Watch these cartoons until I get back." My mother wanted attention. I wanted my mother. *Where is my mother?* She was beginning to seem like a character in someone else's story.

At Blockbuster, I spotted *Suspicion* directed by Alfred Hitchcock and starring Cary Grant and Joan Fontaine. Perfect. I raced down the highway, my headlights beaming through the darkness. Glancing at the clock on the dashboard as I pulled into my mother's driveway, I saw that it was already past eight. I'd have to hurry.

The moment I opened the front door and saw my mother hanging up the phone, I knew I was too late. I clutched the Blockbuster bag.

"He's gone," my mother said.

death

I SANK INTO my father's recliner. All I could think was that I was at Blockbuster getting a movie for my mother when my father died. "Blockbuster," I muttered. I closed my eyes and imagined my father breathing in and out, in and out, finally sliding like a wave to shore, a wave that went further than the other waves until it disappeared.

"You'd better call your sister," I heard my mother say.

I opened my eyes. Dreaming. I must have been dreaming. It felt like the middle of the night.

"And the boys. Call the boys."

I went into my mother's bedroom and rifled through a drawer in the nightstand for her address book. I decided to call my brothers first.

My brother Doug's phone rang and rang. I drifted again, dreaming I couldn't tell anyone. Phones would ring and ring. "Is this the right number?" I hollered to my mother.

"Pammy?" my mother called out, using my childhood name.

"I've been trying to call Doug," I said, walking into the living room where I found my mother staring at a blank TV screen. I put the Hitchcock movie on. "Even if you watch part of it," I said, walking back to the bedroom.

I sat down on the edge of my mother's bed and called Jerry.

"I'm not sure we can get a flight to the viewing," he said.

"He'll only fly on American Airlines is the problem," his wife, Beverly, said.

"Listen, we'll definitely be there for the funeral service. Sounds like you could use some help," he said.

As if he could help. We hadn't talked in years. When I moved to Upstate New York and bought a house, there were more closing fees than I'd planned on and I panicked. I asked this brother-who-had-money to lend me $1500 for a few weeks until I received an income tax refund. What was family for? He wrote back advising me to declare bankruptcy. I was dumbfounded. But I was grateful now during this difficult time that he was offering his support.

"Who was that?" my mother asked.

"Jerry. Jerry and Beverly will come for the funeral."

I tried to call Doug again. No one picked up. I didn't want to leave a message. *Beep:* "Hi, this is Pammy calling to say your— our father—died." I didn't expect he would even miss his father, who never went to see him play hockey in high school and didn't take any interest in him or "the boys." No, I didn't want to leave a message.

I'd have to call my sister now. I'd have to get the call right, say the right thing. I was the one announcing death, not her. She would think she should be the one. She was the oldest. She always took charge.

When Cynthia answered the phone, she sounded annoyed, tense, tired. They would come back in the morning. She gave me some instructions regarding our father's clothes for the viewing. She said she'd call Doug, the brother she was friendly with now. She used to be friendly with Jerry, but she shifted periodically, getting upset with one, then the other.

When I went back into the living room, I found my mother half asleep, gently rocking in her chair, scattering words like seeds: "Yes, it was nice. Very, very nice," she mumbled with a far-away look. A soft smile played across her lips. When I heard "Colonel" in her slur of words, I realized she was thinking about her former boss in a real estate agency where she had worked before she retired and moved to central Florida. The "colonel," as he was called, adored my mother. I had wondered at the time whether they were having an affair.

On screen, Cary and Joan drove off in her car.

"Have you ever been kissed in a car before?"

"Why, Johnny, don't joke with me."

"I'm serious. Would you like to be?"

"Yes."

"Well, well," Johnny said, sweeping the leading lady into his arms.

I guided my mother into her bedroom and helped her into bed. I thought I heard voices in the living room and realized that the movie was still playing. I turned the movie off and sat for a few minutes in my mother's chair, trying to figure out what was going on. I suspected from her mumbling that she'd been at the vodka again. I went into the kitchen and found the bottle under the sink less than half full. I felt angry. I wanted my mother back. This mother was dead drunk, and my father had just died. I was beginning to think "my mother" was a fantasy.

I went back to the living room and pulled the cord to shut the heavy gold drapes over sheer curtains in the picture window, something my father had done at nine every night when he was in this home. Now he was off to a funeral home to be embalmed. The dull, monotonous sound of the cord being pulled was like that of a distant leaf blower droning away, removing debris to reveal what was hidden.

I crawled into bed and collapsed into sleep. That night I dreamed my father called out to me as I hurried down the highway and back. Death, my mother announced when I opened the front door. The scene kept replaying, the door opening and closing with the news until finally the door slammed shut. Startled, I sat up, my fist clenched around a twisted white sheet.

The next morning, I found my mother at the dining room table staring beyond her untouched coffee. She hadn't even brought the newspaper in. She looked stunned. I imagined her wishing she could call her sister Madge, who had been like a mother to her, but Madge had died two years earlier.

I helped her out to her lounge chair on the porch. "I'll handle everything," I said. Trying to keep to her routine, I brought her a cup of fresh coffee, a slice of toast, and the newspaper. "I'm going to get his clothes. When I talked to Cynthia in St. Pete, she told me to air them out."

My mother was engrossed in the newspaper and didn't seem to hear me. "Well, here's a letter to Ann Landers from Aunt Gladys of Orlando," she said without looking up, "complaining about how her children think she's too old to take care of herself. They treat her like a child, though she's perfectly capable. She finds their behavior insulting. Your sister thinks I should go into assisted living. I'm going to show this to her."

I knew she wouldn't dare. She'd tear it out and put it in the drawer with her coupons. But at least she was occupied for now, which gave me a chance to take care of the clothes. I wanted to be sure they were ready when my sister arrived, so there wouldn't be any commotion.

When I returned, my mother had nodded off to sleep. The newspaper had fallen on the floor, but the letter she had torn out was still on her lap. I went out the porch door to the clothesline around the corner and hung out the clothes as if I had just done the washing. His jacket, shirt, and Fruit-of-the-Loom underwear flapped in the breeze.

Leaving my mother to rest, I went back inside and began tidying up the living room. I decided I'd better make a grocery list and went into the kitchen. When I finished the list, I went to the sink to wash the breakfast dishes and again noticed the china cup turned upside down in the drainer. Confused, I looked in the cupboard under the sink and found the vodka bottle in the wastebasket.

I glanced out the window to check on my mother who was sound asleep now. I saw some movement outside. A man and boy, neighbors I guessed, were picking up my father's underwear and jacket off the ground, pinning them back on the line. They must have heard that my father died. What did the man think, seeing a dead man's clothes, his underwear blowing in the breeze? What did he tell the boy?

I decided to put some Indian pudding in the oven before going to the grocery store—five hours in a slow oven to reach perfection. I found the directions in her recipe box. I had added "Very Vermont" to the title, which pleased her. I wondered if my sister would remember the pudding.

Very Vermont Indian Pudding

1-quart milk
½ cup sugar
¼ cup molasses
½ cup yellow corn meal

¼ tsp. cinnamon
1 tsp. salt
2 tbs. butter

Scald 3 cups of the milk and pour over corn meal to which salt has been added. Add molasses, sugar, cinnamon, and butter. Mix thoroughly. Turn into buttered 1½ quart casserole. After the pudding has been in oven 20 minutes, pour in remaining cup of cold milk and stir carefully. Bake in very slow oven (250 degrees) 5-6 hours. Serve warm with whipped cream or vanilla ice cream—or, to be Very Vermont, a slice of butter. Makes 6-8 servings.

Note: To ensure proper consistency, stir carefully four or five times during the first 1½ hours of baking. The pudding is very thin when you put it in the oven, but don't be alarmed—it will thicken and caramelize as it bakes. The long, slow baking is the secret of success with this old-fashioned New England pudding.

let's get this straight

"THE FUNERAL INDUSTRY—I hate the funeral industry," my older sister Cynthia said, standing under the archway that separated the living and dining rooms.

"What's going on?" I asked, putting a bag of groceries on the piano bench. My mother was sitting in the spindle chair next to the piano. She never sat there. She was staring straight ahead, stone-faced. She hadn't even turned her head when I came in.

"They're trying to cheat her," Cynthia said, removing her reading glasses, jostling some papers, squinting at me as if continuing a conversation when she'd only just arrived and we hadn't talked in over a decade.

"The funeral arrangements are paid in full," I said, staring at her, recalling the marked envelope my mother had shown me.

Cynthia was wearing a tailored, powder blue pants suit that matched her eyes. Her face was framed by closely cropped black hair with a hint of gray. She looked younger than her age, ten years younger, like me, and like our mother did until the last couple of years. The women in the family had good genes. The men were balding by thirty.

The black, chunky heel sandals I was wearing added two inches to my five-foot-six-inch height, giving me a six-inch advantage over her "Five Foot Two, Eyes of Blue." My sister would have been sixteen when Dean Martin popularized that song in 1949. She was born in 1933, during the Great Depression; I was born in 1945 at the end of World War II. Now I was fifty and she was sixty-two, but there was more than twelve years and two brothers between us.

"Well, apparently the urn is not included," Cynthia said, walking back into the dining room.

I turned and said to my mother, "Come and sit in your chair." The golden tint in her hazel eyes looked dulled. When I put a hand under her elbow to help her up, she seemed to have shrunk in stature below the five-foot height she claimed to be. She sighed and sunk into her chair, as if to diminish herself. Why was my sister upsetting her like this? Why was she so angry?

Comfort, I imagined, was what my mother wanted. "I'll bring you a cup of tea," I said, moving her small crewel-covered footstool out to the side and putting the 1950s-style flowered TV tray she liked in front of her. "Tea's on its way," I heard myself say with a lilt in my voice, aware it sounded like "Have a nice day." It was the best I could do.

Cynthia looked up from the paperwork and eyed me as I walked past her to put the kettle on. She sat down again at the dining room table to scrutinize the contract. I walked over to the china cabinet and picked out the violet-patterned china cup and turned toward my sister. "Could I have a look?"

"I'll figure it out myself," she said, getting up.

The teakettle screeched.

I walked back into the kitchen and poured some hot water over a Lipton tea bag. I added a little milk and sugar into the tea and brought it to my mother, who used to bring tea and buttered cinnamon-sugared toast to me as a child when I didn't feel well. "I thought you'd like to have your tea in *this* cup," I said, giving the tea a good stir. I put my hand on her hand and said, "Let me know if I can get you anything else."

I wished I could tell my sister that I suspected our mother had been sipping vodka out of this teacup, but I didn't want to betray her. I felt helpless. I was afraid if I tried to reason with my sister, she would erupt and cause a scene. She didn't seem to care at all if she upset *her* mother who seemed different from *my* mother.

Since I couldn't help resolve whatever was going on with my sister in relation to "my" mother, I decided to cook. We would need to eat. This was something I could do. My mother was in no shape to do any cooking and it would keep me out of my sister's way. I decided to make some soup. I chopped some onions and then reached into the fridge for some butter. My mother had half a dozen "I Can't Believe It's Not Butter" containers on the top shelf. "They're great for leftovers," she always said. She liked leftovers for lunch. I wondered which one had "Not Butter." The first one I opened contained cream of celery soup, the second, tuna fish. I lucked out with my third try and started to sauté the onions in the old cast iron frying pan my mother still used.

I wished I could joke with my sister about the "Not Butter" containers and ask her whether she remembered Aunt Madge coming from Boston to visit and how she always brought a cake of butter. "Remember?" I'd say, and we'd laugh like my mother used to do with her sister.

Here was my sister coming into the kitchen now. "Ooogh, onions," she said.

I quickly turned off the burner and headed for the fridge again. I poured two glasses of chilled Napa Chardonnay, my sister's favorite, my mother had told me, and offered her a glass.

"No, I'm on medication and I can feel my blood pressure going up," she said, sitting down at the table again, putting her reading glasses back on to have another look at the papers.

I tried to piece together my sister's heightened anxiety: the death of our father; and my mother had mentioned how stressed she was about her husband's business, which is why they had driven from Long Island, where they were now living, back to Florida where he had established connections. And who knows what else.

My sister took her reading glasses off again and rose to ask, arms crossed now, brows creased, eyes zoomed in for a close-up, "And who—just who do you think you are to arrange our father's funeral?"

For a long moment, our eyes locked. Buddhist nun Pema Chodron appeared over my shoulder, reminding me to pause, not to react right away. *Just breathe.* I regained my composure and decided to try a strategy that I had learned in a compassionate communication workshop. "Cynthia, I feel hurt because I need some recognition for my efforts to be considerate. I told the funeral director that you were in charge and I would have to check with you about details and—"

"*You* feel hurt?" Cynthia scoffed, heading for the porch.

Not wanting my mother to hear us arguing, I followed her.

"Look," she said, turning around to face me, "Mom told me that you blame *me* for her moving to Florida." She paused to be sure that sunk in, then moved closer. "Leaving you all alone in a college dorm room back in Massachusetts. *Let's get this straight.* I told her we were going to move back north—and she came to Florida anyway," she said, backing me against the porch door.

Shocked to learn after decades of assuming that my sister never told my mother that they were moving, that they weren't staying, they wouldn't be around—I stood still as a still life frozen in time. An image of my mother broke my trance: my mother whom I was trying to protect, sitting in her chair sipping a cup of tea, my mother who never corrected me when I said, "I can't believe Cynthia never told you they were leaving," assuming if my mother had known that she wouldn't have fled and abandoned me, which is how it felt at age eighteen.

"I'm going for a walk," I managed to say, staring through my sister. I pushed the screen door open to the wasteland of a landscape in central Florida where my parents had eventually settled. What was my mother doing in this pink petit-four of a house in the middle of nowhere?

"Good. And go for a *long* walk," my sister shouted, slamming the door shut.

zip-a-dee-doo-dah,
zip-a-dee-ay. . .

We all come home and become children again.
—Mimi Schwartz

I WALKED ON a carpet of tough bahiagrass through the neighbors' backyards that bordered the scrub forest nature reserve. "I've been here for two months, helping *our* mother," I wanted to turn around and shout, but I kept walking, heading for the pine grove. Even though my sister's revelation was hurtful and left me feeling betrayed by our mother, the image of her sitting in her chair in the living room hearing her two daughters firing words at each other in a verbal shootout stopped me. She must have had a reason for not telling me that she knew my sister was moving from Miami back to Long Island. When she said after my father's "nervous breakdown" that "a change of scenery would do him good," maybe she meant it would do *her* good. She never talked to me about Turkey Day when everything fell apart. I had to piece together what she left unsaid.

It didn't take long to make the loop. I slowed down and walked off the road, through the prickly pear cacti, toward the railroad track where the Amtrak train whizzed by. What if I jumped a freight train like I'd seen in Westerns on the big blonde TV my parents bought the year Cynthia graduated from high school? I sat down in a pine grove and waited for my sister to leave. I glanced at my watch: 12:20. Cynthia had an appointment with the funeral director at one o'clock. I decided to wait until she drove her Lincoln Town Car out of the driveway. I didn't want to risk another confrontation.

"What should I do?" I asked my ghost of a father.

I am five. I am sitting at the bottom of the stairs playing one of my little yellow 45s on the record player in the brown, faux leather alligator case our mother gave us to share. "Zip-a-dee-doo-dah, zip-a-dee-ay / My, oh my, what a wonderful day." Why not try one of my sister's big, shiny black 78 records stacked in the corner? Just this once. I carefully lift the needle, secure the arm, put the record on and listen to the Andrew Sisters singing, "Hey Daddy, I want a diamond ring, bracelets, everything. / Daddy, you ought to get the best for me, / The best, the very best for me." Then I eye the stack, thinking maybe I have time for one more before my sister gets home—*Crack!* How did it happen that one knee landed on the record, breaking it in two? My head goes spinning round and round like the turntable and at that moment my sister walks in.

"Just whaddya think you're doing?" She grabs the record player, runs past our mother in the kitchen, out the back door, and hurls it down the stairs.

I am six. My sister and her girlfriends walk past me up the stairs to put on their bathing suits. They are going swimming. I hear them talking and laughing as I knock on the closed door. My sister with her breasts stuffed into a red-flowered bikini top cracks the door open to ask what-do-you-want? Oh how I wanted to go with them. My sister does not want me in the room and doesn't want me tagging along on their outing, but she gives in after I plead: "Won't you take me to the quarry with you, pleeez? Sister-sister, won't you pulleeez?" Sitting at the edge of Red Rock Quarry in my baggy shorts and halter top, breasts flat as pancakes, I look up at the older girls stretched out on rocks, hoping their upturned breasts are being stared at.

I am nine. I hear shuffling, then muffled voices in the kitchen, something about how my sister has run away. But where would she be running to? It is some time before I learn that Cynthia has run away and gotten married and a long time before I learned that she *had* to get married and a still longer time before I learn exactly what that means: that there isn't going to be a wedding in the garden and my mother won't be making her a white satin gown.

Now like a spy, I watch my sister reach into her shiny navy blue shoulder bag for her sunglasses, open the car door, adjust the rearview mirror. "Oh no!" I exclaim, standing up, suddenly remembering that I had hung our father's funeral clothes on the line "to air them" as she had told me to do. Would she remember? As if my sister heard me, she opened the car door again, went back inside the house, and returned with the clothes. Was my mother already in the car?

I waited until the car was out of sight and then went back into the house.

days of our lives

It isn't a matter of whether you can go home again. You just do. Language, that most ghostly kind of travel, hands out the tickets.

—Patricia Hampl

WHEN I OPENED the front door, I was startled to see the TV on and my mother in her chair watching the soap opera *Days of Our Lives*.

"Cynthia thought it best I stay here," my mother explained, putting down half a grilled cheese sandwich on her TV tray. "Come on in," she said, waving as if I'd just happened to be passing by. "Would you like some lunch?" she asked me who all these days had been asking her.

"No, I'm not hungry," I said, sitting down on the piano bench, staring across the room to the picture window, as if it were a screen on which I could project my mind at work trying to connect the past with the present. I felt I was reliving one of my sister's angry outbursts, only this time I was thrown out the porch door instead of the record player.

I glanced at my mother, her eyes focused on the drama unfolding onscreen: a confrontation between two sisters in a fictional family. I turned and looked at high school graduation photos of my sister and me, placed on end tables on either side of the floral-patterned couch. They were separated by a row of my mother's hand-sewn "happy dolls," as I called them, seated along the top edge. "I thought I'd better leave, get out of her way," I said to my mother while gazing at my sister, stilled in the photo. I didn't understand why she was so angry.

"I would've done the same. Your father wouldn't like this one bit," she said, going for her Lipton Cup-a-Soup.

"She doesn't want me here. If you were in my place, what would you do?"

A glint in her eyes. "I don't go where I'm not wanted," my mother said, looking up from her soup. "If a person does not welcome you or listen to you, leave and shake the dust off your feet. That's either Matthew or Mark," she said.

"What are you talking about?" I asked, standing up.

"I know," she said, a little excited. "You could go to a motel for the weekend."

"A motel?" I repeated, thinking I hadn't heard right.

"I know just the one, the one near your father's favorite restaurant. You can have breakfast there in the morning and come to the viewing later and the funeral the next day."

I felt confused, disoriented, unable to process, as if my mother had gone missing and this one had been sent in as a replacement.

"You'd better hurry," my mother said, getting up to peer through the sheer curtains in the picture window. "She won't be long. She forgot his shoes."

"The shoes?" I screeched like the teakettle.

"Yes, the ones he wore at the nursing home. I gave all the others away. He'd only wear those old scruffy ones in the end, those ones that clicked when he walked, remember?"

I remembered only too well. "Well, he can't wear—wait. His feet won't show."

"Oh, that's right," my mother said, sitting back down in front of the TV.

I pictured my father all dressed up with a jacket and tie—and no shoes.

"Well, you'd better pack," my mother said matter-of-factly. "It's a shame you have to pay to stay somewhere when you've a perfectly good room here."

I headed for the guest room. I had become a child again. I did as I was told. I went into the closet, pulled out a suitcase and started packing.

"Sorry, we're closed," an onscreen voice called out from the soap opera that still played, as if nothing were happening here and now in this family, in this house.

"Guess I was misinformed," another voice replied.

"'Closed' means closed, even for you," the first voice retaliated, "especially for you."

"You'll need to turn the oven off in an hour or so," I reminded my mother, who had come into the room. "The Indian pudding, remember?" She nodded. "And don't tell Cynthia where I am," I said as if we were in cahoots.

"Listen," I said, motioning my mother to sit down on the edge of a bed. "Your best behavior, understand?"

"Yes, boss," she said with a wry smile, as if this were a game.

"You can't have anything to drink."

My mother nodded.

"If you fall down again, Cynthia will send you to assisted living—I'm warning you."

valentino

I OPENED THE door to motel room 123, a room in the back where I was the only occupant in a long row of rooms. I didn't know what to do. It wasn't as if I were traveling and this was an overnight rest stop. I felt as if I had been transported to a 1950s Hollywood set. People in my family were behaving very strangely and while my father had died—that was a fact—everything else seemed like fiction.

Dazed, I went out on the cement slab of a porch in front of my room, pulled up a metal chair with a tacked-on plywood seat, and propped the faded aqua-colored door open just enough so the apartment dwellers across the street couldn't see in.

What would they see? A tattered, bent lampshade; a stained, torn bedspread; untold stories from the 1950s when people traveled the old road to Miami. What they would see was my long, black cotton funeral dress batiked with swirls of aqua hanging in an open closet on a rickety metal pole. I felt abandoned: this motel room, that dorm room. Suddenly I was back in college again.

What I saw was a still life of my dearly departed father, alone now, out of reach. The picture faded as I lowered myself into the chair. I slid the palms of my hands over my eyes and cheeks, pushing back some strands of hair, and slipped on my Valentino sunglasses. A woman wearing Valentino sunglasses does not get thrown out of the house.

The phone rang. It was my mother. "I suppose you'll be taking in men all night," she joked. "Your sister's always been jealous of you. I told her you went to a motel. Wouldn't say where," my mother continued as if this were matter-of-fact normal.

"Where's Cynthia?" I asked, sitting down on the edge of the bed.

"You stay put," my mother said. "I'll see you at the viewing tomorrow afternoon."

Puzzled about my mother's response, I put the phone down, removed my sunglasses, and stared out the open door. The sun was about to set. I noticed a road next to the apartment building across the street. I'll take a walk. Walk it off, I thought with a smile, as if I could.

Pine trees gave way to Valencia Acres, a cluster of mobile homes resembling New England-style clapboard houses. TIENDA MEXICANA LA GLORIA, a sign on a grocery store read, followed by WE SELL BEER ON SUNDAY and WE WIRE MONEY. Across the street, two scruffy-looking young men eyed me suspiciously. I looked away. The houses became smaller. Several old trailers had been abandoned in a field. I glanced up to see three men sitting on a fence, three beautiful brown backs in a row. I smiled as the men turned and waved.

The road dead-ended at a cemetery. In the distance, I saw a red pickup truck and a man digging a grave. He was wearing a white tee and black baseball cap and jeans and white sneakers. "A modern gravedigger," I said out loud. The sign on the gate read NO TRESPASSING. I turned around for the walk back to the motel. On the side of the road, I saw a newly dead cottontail rabbit looking restful, as if it had just been stuffed. I shuddered to think of my father being embalmed for the viewing.

I heard a faint sound, an accordion sound, something polka-like, festive. As I got closer, I recognized that it was a mariachi band. A handsome young man was standing in the doorway of a house, his long black hair framing a smile. I was desperate for conversation.

Later that night I dreamed he said, "Come in," as if I were an expected guest. "We are about to cut my father's birthday cake. You are just in time." I followed him through the front door and out the back, where a crowd was gathered around a table and a mariachi band was playing a Mexican birthday song—"'Las Mananitas', you know it?" he asked. Before I could reply, violins began to serenade his father. A man in a wide-brimmed sombrero sang a verse and everyone joined in the chorus. *"Felicidades a mi papa,"* my new friend shouted as his father cut the first slice of cake. The band broke into "Mucha Muchacha": *"Mucha Muchacha . . . Mucha Muchacha . . . Cha- cha! Cha! Cha!"* I drank a margarita and ate some tortilla chips dipped into freshly made salsa, as I wandered around the celebration in this chili pepper-lit space at sundown.

His father welcomed me, cut me a piece of cake, and thanked me for coming. Guests smiled and nodded. I felt as if I belonged. I thanked the man who had kindly invited me in. "It's dark. It's getting late," he said. "I'll walk with you."

We talked enough for him to know I was sad that I hadn't been with my father at the end, that no one was with him, that he had died alone and now I was alone and confused about my sudden, unexpected displacement—my sister's strange behavior and my mother's odd complicity. Toward the end of the walk, he held my hand as if offering his condolences.

We sat outside on the cement slab of motel room 123 and drank tequila out of two plastic cups. The rhythm of our conversation slowed and finally there was no sound, only space. The moon was partially illuminated. I spread my fingers lightly over his lips, as if to say "no words." When I removed my hand, he moved closer and kissed me gently. Then he was gone.

the viewing

WHEN I WALKED into the funeral home, I was surprised to see my mother stretched out on a couch by the door. One foot was bandaged and propped up; the other was tucked into a powder blue slipper-bootie. The main room was crowded with neighbors from Sun Ray Homes. I watched them greet my mother and then move on to the viewing room.

Doug hugged me hard. I looked at him in his white T-shirt and jeans. "No time to change," he said, as if he had read my mind. "Had to take her to Emergency. Get her ankle X-rayed. She fought with the doctor. Screamed 'Give me those pain pills!' He told her to go home and take Tylenol. It took all I had to get her here." We both looked over at her on the couch. "And she's mad at Jim. Said he called her a drug addict. They're not speaking." Doug told me he didn't want to get involved, which is just what our father would have said.

Aunt Madge's son Wayne, who had driven from Atlanta, stopped to ask what had happened to his favorite aunt. I heard Doug start telling a sanitized version of the story. I eyed my sister glaring at our mother, saying too loudly, "Look at her," pointing with her chin. "You'd think it was *her* funeral." The neighbors looked stunned. They loved my mother.

My mother was talking cheerily to Cousin Wayne. She caught my glimpse and shrugged, as if she couldn't begin to explain.

I headed for the viewing room, but my sister stopped me in the doorway. "And where were *you* last night?" she asked, chin up, her eyes squinting head on. "Running away like that. I heard you went to Orlando."

"Orlando?" I turned away and walked down the aisle, quickening my pace.

My father was laid out for viewing in a half-closed casket on a dark red velvet platform. Jerry had made his appearance through the lone bouquet of flowers next to the casket. In his coat and tie, my father looked like he did when he posed for that ad in *Hardware Age* magazine. But he was so alone up there, so removed. Someone had folded his hands in prayer.

I needed to sit down, but where would I sit? I saw Cynthia and Jim seated in the first row, Doug and Nancy in the second. With my head down, I walked back down the aisle and settled into a pew in the last row. I wanted to cover my eyes with my hands and peek out like a child at my father laid out for viewing. My father wouldn't like this one bit. He never liked an argument.

Someone wheeled my mother down the center aisle and helped her into a seat in the second row. My sister-in-law came back and sat down beside me. For the first time, I felt some relief, a hand over my hand, tears rolling down my cheeks. I hadn't wanted to part with him like this. I was glad I kissed his forehead when he lay dying in the nursing home.

Nancy said that they would take my mother home and then they were going out to dinner to talk about what to do about *her.* "We need you to go back to the house tonight."

I looked at her with a puzzled expression. She hadn't come to comfort me. I felt abandoned, just like I did on Turkey Day. Dreaming, I must be dreaming. It was as if our lives were being scripted for a series of episodes on *Days of Our Lives*.

"Your mother took a lot of sleeping pills," she said. "We don't know how many. She keeps them hidden in her pocketbook. And some vodka Jim had left in her bedroom closet—gone. Your brother found her this morning on all fours. On her hands and knees heading for the kitchen. She couldn't walk. She said her arthritis was acting up."

Hearing that familiar last line, my eyes widened, as unfortunately I did understand, and more than I wanted to confess.

"There's more," she said. "She messed in her bed, too. Sheets all twisted."

"Wait!" I said, opening my eyes, staring at her.

"And you should've seen your sister," she said as if she hadn't heard.

"Do you mean—" My mouth snapped open as if more air were required. "Do you mean Cynthia didn't stay with her last night? *No one stayed with her?*

i'm so glad you're here

I CHECKED OUT of the motel. On the drive back to my mother's house, I thought about my mother being left alone all night. I felt guilty. Why did I leave and go to a motel? Why didn't my mind say, "Your mother is not herself right now—don't listen to her"? My sister knew I was gone. My mother said she told her I went to a motel. Why didn't someone stay with her?

I pulled into the driveway and opened the door to find my mother sitting at the dining room table with her foot propped up on a chair. "They asked me to come back and stay with you," I said, putting down my suitcase.

She smiled and said, "I'm so glad you're here."

I sat down at the table. "Are you hungry?"

"I'm starved."

"I'll make us some grilled cheese sandwiches," I said, helping her into the living room. "He used to watch the evening news while you were getting dinner ready, remember?" She nodded as I settled her into her chair.

I glanced at the TV Guide. "How about the news followed by *Jeopardy* and then Lawrence Welk?" I turned on the TV and gave my mother the remote control.

"We'll get your foot X-rayed again next week," I said, propping my mother's foot on the footrest.

We often had grilled cheese sandwiches on Sunday nights in the kitchen, just the three of us after my three older siblings had left home. The meal was lighter because of the wonderful home-cooked dinner my mother served after church on Sundays. Sometimes my father would suggest we eat at the Bridge View Grill that looked out over the Connecticut River.

Going into the kitchen, I sighed with relief to be alone with my mother. I reached into the refrigerator for some slices of Wonder Bread and what had become known as "American" cheese, a processed cheese product manufactured by Kraft in individual slices wrapped in plastic. I no longer ate Wonder Bread, but on this night I made grilled cheese sandwiches 1950s style and poured two glasses of Cara Cara orange juice.

While our sandwiches were frying in my mother's old cast iron skillet, I took out another TV tray and put it in front of my father's recliner. I placed our sandwiches on small pale green plastic plates and added a couple slices of dill pickle, as my mother used to do. "Guess they're out having drinks and dinner somewhere," I said as I sat in my father's chair.

"Plans for sending US troops to Bosnia will go into effect immediately if a peace agreement is not reached," CBS news anchor Dan Rather announced.

"Looks like another war," my mother said. "Where's Bosnia?"

"National parks and monuments will re-open Monday after a six-day government shut down," Dan Rather continued.

"Tomorrow's his funeral service," my mother said as if worried the shutdown might be extended another day and somehow delay the service.

Co-anchor Connie Chung reported that Princess Diana admitted during a BBC interview that she had been unfaithful to Prince Charles.

"I read somewhere that she had an affair with her riding instructor," my mother said, finishing her grilled cheese.

"I'll do the dishes, clean up the kitchen."

"Oh, good, *Jeopardy*'s coming on," she said as I took the dishes away.

That night I helped my mother into bed and sat with her until she drifted off to sleep. Then I went back to the living room and sat down again in my father's recliner. While my mother had removed his pipe rack, she'd kept his amber glass tobacco jar on the side table. When I lifted the pewter lid embossed with flowers and leaves, the smell of cherry tobacco took me back to a childhood memory: my father smoking his pipe while he pushed me on a tree swing just beyond his "cherry orchard," as he called the four cherry trees he'd planted between his garden and the path to the woods. I put the lid back on, sunk back in his chair, and thought of my father in a casket. Then I got up and walked over to the picture window and pulled the heavy gold drapes shut.

the service

THE NEXT MORNING, Jerry and his wife stood at the door with a box of Dunkin' Donuts and four cups of coffee. "We're here," he said, greeting our mother as she hobbled into the living room. He helped her to a chair in the dining room and offered her some coffee. "We'll take you to the funeral service. We'll go together," he said.

Jerry stopped me before I got into the car. "Wait," he said, his hand cupping my elbow, "I've been wanting to tell you I was wrong. What I did was wrong. I could've given you the money. That wasn't it. But I earned my money the hard way. I worked hard, and I thought I'd teach you a lesson—teach you to stand on your own two feet."

I looked down at my feet, and we both burst out laughing. "Well, I don't think that was ever a problem," I declared. "My feet were always too big for me growing up." *Hey Big Feet. Canoe foot! Hahaha . . .*

"I was wrong," he repeated, looking right into my eyes.

I looked back. I believed him.

"You've grown into your feet," he teased, as I ducked my head into the rental car, two inches taller—five foot eight with my black silk hat on. I smiled, pleased at a break from tension, until the car

71

pulled up to the curb at the funeral home and my sister gave me her what-do-you-think-you're-doing look.

The casket was closed. Someone read the Twenty-third Psalm.

The Lord is my shepherd; I shall not want. . . .

Someone sang "I Love to Tell the Story."

I love to tell the story
  Because I know 'tis true;
  It satisfies my longings
    As nothing else can do. . . .

Then came a little talk by the funeral director about loving your brothers and sisters and the good fortune that we could all be together. I didn't dare turn my head to look at my sister.

In the foyer after the service, Wayne asked me if everyone was going back to the house. I knew he had been looking forward to spending some time with Cynthia and Doug, who were closest to him in age. "No," I said. He nodded as if he understood. What he understood was that something had gone horribly wrong.

flounder florentine

MY FATHER DIED on Friday evening, November 17, 1995; the viewing was Sunday, the 19th; the funeral service, Monday, the 20th. My sister and her husband and my older brother Doug and his wife did not come back to the house after the service to eat and share memories, which was devastating for my mother. Fortunately, Cousin Wayne and my other brother Jerry and his wife came. The five of us ate Flounder Florentine that I made, following a recipe from the Moosewood Restaurant, a longtime vegetarian restaurant in Ithaca, New York. I made an exception to my vegetarian diet—as did the Moosewood.

Flounder Florentine

Spinach, dill, and almonds are the grace notes to the flounder here, one of our most popular dishes.

2 tbs. vegetable oil or butter

¼ to ½ cup toasted almonds, finely chopped

¼ cup finely chopped onions

10 oz. fresh spinach, stemmed and chopped

1 tsp. fresh lemon juice

1 tbs. fresh dill (1 tsp. dried)

2 lb. flounder fillets

Sauté the onions in the butter or oil until translucent. Add the chopped spinach and the dill and cook covered until the spinach is wilted. Remove from the heat, add the almonds and lemon juice, and allow to cool.

Rinse the flounder. Place each fillet, skinned side up, flat on a board. Spoon a small amount of the spinach filling onto each fillet and then roll it up. Place the rolled fish in an oiled baking pan and bake covered at 375 degrees for 20 to 25 minutes, until the fish is tender and flaky.

We sat around the dining table in silence except for the perfunctory "pass the butter" comments. No one asked why the rest of the family did not join us. My mother gazed off into the distance as if no one were there.

Midway through the meal, Wayne looked across at my mother pushing her food around her plate like a child. "You were my favorite aunt," he said. "I spent the best time of my childhood at your house."

What he didn't say was what I knew, that the reason he came to my father's funeral was not because of his memories of my father (which would have been of him sitting in his chair, no doubt)— no, it was because he wanted to be with my mother and with my two oldest siblings and yes, he had expected to be with them at the family gathering. He was not only disappointed but also confused. Then he left. Then Jerry left with his wife to catch a plane. And I was left with my mother again.

I thought I would be so glad to have my mother to myself and without the complications of her relationship with my father. But over the weekend and gradually over my stay, I had come to realize that my mother was now this mother, that the mother I had been attached to by an umbilical cord on the inside and by an invisible golden thread on the outside during my childhood had changed over the years through all that life presented, including the long aftermath of my father's breakdown. This was my mother after all.

turkey day 2

IT WAS MY mother's eighty-sixth birthday and only days after my father had been carried out on a stretcher, this time to be embalmed and displayed for a final viewing. No one called or sent flowers or cards. My mother didn't say anything about the phone or the doorbell not ringing. I parted the sheer curtains in the picture window and watched her go to the mailbox and return empty handed. She stood in the doorframe for a moment and turned to look at me. Her hazel eyes were dark hollows; her face was pale. She was heartbroken, my mother. My father would have been upset to see her like this.

"I'll take you to dinner tonight," I said, as if a nice dinner out would cheer her up. "It's your birthday," I reminded her. "We're not staying here." I crossed the room to put my arm around her and walked with her out to the chaise lounge on the porch. She was asleep by the time I finished making a reservation.

I went back into the living room and sat in my father's recliner. I felt disoriented as if I'd had a bad dream. From my siblings' point of view, my mother had behaved badly.

"Sheets all twisted, on all fours headed for the kitchen."

"Probably to hide that bottle of vodka."

"Mixing drugs and drink."

"Shameful."

"You'd think it was her funeral, the way she greeted everyone, laid out on a couch at the entrance."

My sister and her husband wanted nothing to do with her—or me. Wait, did they think I was to blame because I didn't stay the night with her? It wasn't my idea to leave the house, but I fell under my mother's spell and went to the motel.

The old adage "beware of assumptions" came to mind. I assumed that my sister or someone would stay with her. Where did Cynthia get the idea that I went to Orlando? And if she believed I took off, wouldn't she worry about our mother being left alone that night? When my mother called me at the motel, she joked with me. She didn't sound disturbed. Why wasn't I suspicious?

It's true that my mother would not have gotten into that disastrous state had I been with her that night. I concluded I was responsible for the way the weekend turned out. But my sister (I go on, trying to reason) was angry when she arrived after our father died. She was on a rant about the funeral industry while my mother, still in shock, sat stone-faced, a look that was repeated when no one stayed or called after the funeral. I didn't understand why my sister was acting like this. Could I have done something different?

My mother and I went to a restaurant in Sebring and had a lovely meal. I arranged to have a little cake brought to the table, which surprised and pleased her. A family at a nearby table sang "Happy Birthday."

When we got home, my mother told me she wanted to make Thanksgiving dinner the next day.

"The whole meal?"

"Yes," she said.

"But no one's coming."

She told me that she had bought two Cornish hens in place of a turkey.

"But I'm vegetarian."

"Well, you can eat the stuffing. You always liked my stuffing," she said. I understood that she needed to go through this important ritual.

We rose early and worked all morning so we could have Thanksgiving dinner at 1:00 p.m.: cranberry sauce, green beans, and hollowed-out Cara Cara oranges filled with mashed sweet potatoes topped with pecans. Neither of us could eat. I pulled a little stuffing out of the hen's cavity, its legs up in the air like exclamation points. I imagined turning it over and giving it back its feet and watching it run along the Cornish coast.

I looked over at my mother who was busy carving off a leg. "What lovely leftovers," she said, getting up to clear the table.

x-ray

THE NEXT WEEK I took my mother to have her foot X-rayed again. She looked sprightly, my mother, dressed in a bluebell-flowered blouse and sky blue polyester pants as if this were a special occasion, lunch at a nice restaurant, perhaps. She sauntered into the office, her cane synchronized with the sprained ankle.

"Beautiful day today," a middle-aged man said to my mother as we sat down.

"Yes, and after that rainstorm we had yesterday afternoon," my mother said, as if comforted to be talking about the weather again. Then came the usual exchange about injuries.

"What happened to you?" my mother asked. "That's quite a boot you have there. Did you break your leg?"

He told her that he fractured his foot when he fell down some stairs. "Going to get the cast off today, I hope. What about you?" he asked, glancing at her blue slipper-bootie.

My mother told him that she tripped and sprained her ankle. "Sometimes I don't look where I'm going," she said with a twinkle in her eye.

The man laughed.

"I'm eighty-six," she said, as if that were an excuse, or perhaps to invite the predictable response.

"You're kidding," he said. "You're eighty-six? Well, you get around very well, even with that foot," the man said.

I turned to look at my mother. And my mother winked at me as if we were in cahoots.

i took my mother to church

A FEW WEEKS after my father's funeral, some neighbors stopped by to see how my mother was doing. "You need to get out of the house," one neighbor said to my mother sitting in her rocking chair in the living room opposite my father's empty recliner. "The church has lots of social activities," another neighbor said cautiously.

At the mention of "church," my mother turned her head and peered through the sheer curtains of the picture window: drifting, it looked to me looking at her, as if trying to tune in what she'd all these years tried to tune out. After my father had a "nervous breakdown," my mother stopped going to the northern Baptist church. She was deeply hurt that the pastor of the church, where my father had served as a deacon and my mother had been active in the women's group, had not reached out to her "in time of need," was how she put it.

"Have you two had dinner yet?" her neighbor Nell asked me. In fact, we hadn't. Neither of us had any appetite.

"Helen, dear, you might enjoy a church dinner," Nell said, crossing the room and placing her hand on my mother's hand to get her attention. "We've just come from one—a spaghetti supper put on by the men of the church."

The corners of my mother's lips turned up ever so slightly at the thought of men cooking dinner.

Nell sat down on the hassock in front of my father's recliner and turned to me, sitting on the piano bench. "The dinner was sooo good," Nell said. "Why not head over and get a ticket?"

Another neighbor rose and went over to my mother: "Honey, I'm tellin' ya, it is gooood. The man who makes the sauce is a chef. That sauce—so delicious. And the bread. Italian bread loaded with garlic, lightly toasted."

My mother looked over at me to signal it was time. I rose and thanked everyone for stopping by.

"Shall we try it?" I asked my mother when they left.

"Can it be that goood if they are serving a hundred people?"

It was a little after six o'clock. We agreed we needed to eat something.

What we got was a huge helping of overcooked spaghetti and some doctored-up Ragu-type sauce with ground hamburger thrown in and butter-soaked bread with no taste of garlic and a tiny salad with some bottled French dressing. We played with our food like children trying to get out of eating something we didn't like. My mother ate a slice of some box-mix yellow cake with prepared chocolate frosting, which cost an extra $4.50, she complained on the way out. No one talked to us beyond an initial "hello" greeting. They were mostly northerners reuniting, same time, same place, see you next year.

I rose early the next morning, Sunday morning, and walked to the scrub nature reserve to view the sunrise. When I looked up at the vast skyscape—a canvas strewn with gradations of pink-colored, textured clouds against an ever-brightening blue—my perspective opened like a prayer plant whose leaves fold up at night and unfold in the morning to catch as much sunlight as possible.

Then I took my mother to church. I don't know how I convinced her to go to the Sunday service—or myself. I had stopped going to church when I went to college. But I was leaving at the end of the month. Except for conversations with a few neighbors, my mother's social life this past year had been confined to residents and staff at the nursing home. This church was the only social center in the community and I thought it was worth a try.

"I can't stand this," my mother whispered to me partway through the service. "Let's get out of here."

Awkward with her cane, she would draw attention, and Nell and her husband sitting next to her would be startled.

I pointed to the sermon to come, "Refocusing Your Life," and gave my mother the elbow.

She rolled her eyes.

We left.

the white cliffs of dover

AFTER MY FATHER died, I stayed with my mother through Christmas and invited her to visit me in London, where I would be teaching for the spring semester.

"Why, I couldn't do that," she said when I proposed that she come in March. My mother had never been outside New England, except to go to Florida, and had never imagined going abroad to old England.

"Why not? You're a free woman now," I teased. I saw just enough glint in her eyes to encourage me to call Aunt Peggy, a veteran world traveler and a "free woman" since George, my mother's brother, had died. She and my mother had remained close friends. Peggy flew from Upstate New York to visit her every year.

No, Aunt Peggy hadn't made any travel plans yet, she told us when we phoned her. Yes, she'd love to accompany my mother to London.

I took a taxi to Gatwick airport to meet my mother and aunt rather than trying to catch a train to Victoria station and switch to the Underground and deal with their luggage. I had suggested my mother purchase a new suitcase she could pull easily, but she insisted on using the powder blue suitcase, circa 1950, that her sister Madge had given her. The taxi driver waited with me behind the rope railing at International Arrivals, so he could help with the baggage.

"Is that your mother? That one?" He pointed, as if I were being shown a lineup of suspects and asked to express any hint of recognition. Then he gave up and went for coffee while the meter ticked away. After an hour, it occurred to me that my mother and aunt were waiting inside for me to meet them. My aunt's world travel was always organized through some tour. On her own, my aunt perhaps did not realize that they needed to go through customs first. It took me another half hour to find some official who would believe my story and go find them and walk them through. Soon they arrived, grinning with embarrassment. My mother, wearing wide, aqua polyester pants, said that they had wondered what was taking me so long. Eighty English pounds lighter, we were in my flat.

When they woke up and got dressed the next morning, my mother and her sister-in-law found themselves wearing the same style sweater in different colors. That moment turned into "The Sweater Girls" photo I took of them on the balcony. My mother looked frail from the journey and changes in her life.

We took taxis everywhere: to St. Paul's Cathedral, the Tower of London, and to high tea at Claridge's Hotel in Mayfair, until my mother decided it was too expensive and, yes, she could handle the Underground. "Mind the gap," she'd say to my aunt. How thrilled they were to ride on a double-decker sightseeing bus and visit Harrods and Kew Gardens. They also loved shopping in the small stores they could walk to in the Little Venice neighborhood where I was living.

The highlight of their visit was going on a road trip with my students to see the White Cliffs of Dover. They sat behind the driver in the front seat with a large window view, waiting, waiting for them to come into view. My mother wore her aqua polyester pants, her "Florida pants" (I called them), and her "sweater girl" sweater. I sat in the front seat opposite them. When the cliffs came into view, the two of them burst out singing, "There'll be bluebirds over / The white cliffs of Dover / Tomorrow, just you wait and see / There'll be love and laughter / And peace ever after . . . "

The students began clapping. None of us understood what the song meant to them. I later learned that the lyrics, written by American composers Nat Burton and Walter Kent in 1941, looked toward a time when WWII would be over and peace would rule over the iconic white cliffs. Ironically, the writers had never been to Dover and were unaware that bluebirds were not native to England. The song, which was popularized by British singer Vera Lynn's recording in 1942, signifies happiness and well-being. I imagine this song lifted my mother's spirits both back then and at this time in her life.

This travel adventure of a lifetime was a break for my mother. Still, she could not understand why my sister and her husband had turned on her the weekend of my father's funeral. Though she didn't say, I caught her drift, so to speak, as I watched her looking out the window, letting her hurt rise, then tucking it back in as we sat together in the kitchen early in the morning.

I had written a letter from London to my sister about how our mother had been affected by her behavior and pleaded with her to make peace. Her response: "What do you think you're doing sending me a letter like this?"

What would I tell my mother? I had shown her the letter before I sent it and she approved. "Very good," she said. When my mother came into the kitchen for a cup of tea, I told her my sister hadn't liked the letter. I didn't show my mother her response; instead, I burst into song: "There'll be bluebirds over / The white cliffs of Dover / Tomorrow, just you wait and see..."

heartache

The ground is always shifting. Nothing lasts, including us.
—Pema Chodron

THE FOLLOWING DECEMBER my mother called to ask if I would visit her during my winter break. "*Please* come," she said, sounding desperate again, and I was worried.

When I arrived, I found my mother anxious about a visit my sister was planning in April. When Cynthia called, she had not mentioned what happened the weekend of the funeral, and my mother couldn't express her deep-felt hurt. Her buried pain was unspeakable.

After my arrival, I went with my mother to visit an old friend. He told her that she should tell her daughter that she did not want her to visit. "Not after what happened," he said. "You should tell her," he repeated, putting his hand over her hand. While I sensed my mother thought he was right, I also knew she could neither handle confrontation nor pretend that she was not hurt. She wrestled with this problem for days. Her anxiety mounted.

"My stomach," my mother said, late one night a week into my visit. Her face suddenly paled as if she were about to faint. The phone rang and I answered it.

My mother looked at me inquisitively. "It's Uncle Webb," I said.

My father's brother was calling from Massachusetts to see how my mother was doing. She sat down and put one hand on her stomach and with the other reached for the phone.

"Do you think you should take this call?" I asked. "I think I should drive you to Emergency."

No, she would take the call, she told me as if this were a question of etiquette. She didn't say a word to Uncle Webb about how she was feeling. By the time she got off the phone, she said she was okay, she'd be okay. "No need to drive to Emergency," she said.

My daughter Angela had called a couple days before to ask if she could spend the weekend with us. She was on winter break from college and had found a cheap flight to Orlando. "I just feel like I want to be with you and Gran," she said.

On Saturday while we three had lunch together on the porch, my mother said again that she didn't feel well, that she guessed she'd go to her bedroom and rest a little.

"I'll do the dishes," I said.

Angela went to sit by her. I was just finishing up when my daughter came in to tell me that "Gran seems *really* sick." When I walked into her room, her face was pale again and she was gripping her stomach.

Angela and I got her into the car, and I drove as fast as I could the ten miles to Emergency. "Her stomach again," I was thinking. The last time she had this problem, the doctor said there was nothing he could do. Adhesions from several operations were cemented together.

When we checked her in, she handed me her oversized pocketbook. "Everything's in there," she said, as the nurse put her in a wheelchair and took her away. We sat down and waited.

Everybody knows you always wait in Emergency, but after well over an hour and seeing no one else waiting, I rose, clutching my mother's pocketbook. "Maybe they are helping others with more serious problems," I said to my daughter. "I'll go and inquire."

"Your mother had a massive heart attack," the nurse behind the desk said. "*Massive*," she repeated to be sure I understood. She said that I should have called an ambulance, that they could have started trying to revive her sooner. I was stunned. How would this help now? She raised her brows, as if dismissing me as hopeless. "You'll get to go in soon," she said, her head down now, her eyes glued to her paperwork.

I told my daughter what I had learned and we sat down to wait. As I tried to steady my trembling self, I thought of my insistence that my mother wear an emergency alert necklace "that protects seniors when family cannot be with them," whether if she had been alone, she would have pushed the button that would have sent paramedics on their way, whether she would have been better off if she had been alone. But the truth is she wouldn't have sounded the alarm—she wouldn't have worn that necklace. That necklace was for me to feel I was taking care of my mother. Admittedly, it was also an alternative to the assisted living my sister had proposed, which had upset my mother, for she could take care of herself, thank you.

Soon another nurse led us down a corridor and paused outside my mother's room. "They managed to revive her," the nurse said, putting her hand on mine.

I smiled to see my mother and teased her that she'd had a massive heart attack. "Massive," I repeated, as if going all out was impressive. She smiled to see me as I bent over and kissed her forehead and told her I loved her. Then she reached to shake the doctor's hand. "Dr. Lopez, I believe we have met before," she said cordially with a twinkle in her eye.

"It's good to see you again," the doctor whispered warmly, his eyes brightened by her voice as if they were old friends and it had been a lifetime since they had seen each other. He put his chart down and held her eyes with his eyes while he slowly reached to hold her offered hand as if to say, "Welcome back."

Then he called me over to the end of her bed where he picked up her chart again and explained that she would be going to intensive care. "The only thing," he said, and just as he was about to explain what could go wrong, my mother screamed and threw her hand over her heart as if stabbed. When I turned and clenched the doctor's shoulders with both hands and shouted, "*Do something! Give her something!*" her pocketbook fell to the floor.

The doctor gave her a shot and the nurses shuttled us out of the room while they tried to revive her again. When a priest instead of a nurse appeared in the Emergency waiting room, I knew she was "gone," as my mother would say. My daughter pressed her hand into my thigh as if to brace me.

"I'm sorry," the priest said, guiding me to an office to sign some papers and address the sensitive subject of the body: Would there be a viewing? Did I want her embalmed? Cremated? "It's a time-sensitive matter," he said. "Do you want to see her?" he asked.

I went into the room where my mother's body laid waiting, still warm, and kissed her again on her forehead.

Her last memory of her own mother had been when she was five and her older sister Beatrice took her into the parlor of their Vermont home where their mother was laid out for the viewing. She had lifted my mother up and told her to kiss Mama. *Kiss her,* she said. And my mother did as she was told and then she screamed and screamed. Which is why I went back to kiss my mother's forehead, to honor the pain she carried her whole life.

good luck with your sister

I WALKED OUT of the hospital with my mother's pocketbook, my daughter trailing behind me. We didn't speak on the ten-mile drive back to my mother's house. There was too much to process and nowhere to begin. I parked my mother's car in the driveway, and we walked up the sidewalk and stood on the pink flamingo welcome mat. The door was locked. My mother wasn't home. Keychain in hand, I found the key and opened the door. I put the pocketbook on the seat of the rocking chair where my mother always sat and walked into the kitchen to call my siblings.

I sat down by the wall phone and paused, trying to prepare myself. A little over a year ago when I called my siblings to tell them our father died, I called my sister last. This time I decided to call my sister first.

Cynthia wanted to know what happened at the hospital.

"Did you tell the doctor to look at her chart?"

"Her chart? There was no time," I said.

"I'm sure it was on her record that she was allergic to morphine." My sister didn't understand that there was no what-to-do pause. Death happened in a nanosecond.

91

"The doctor told me her death was caused by a blocked artery," I said calmly. I didn't want an argument.

My sister said that she and her husband would drive down from Long Island.

My mother had designated Doug executor of her will. He and his wife would fly down the next morning. Jerry and his wife would not be coming. They would send flowers. I recalled Jerry saying to me the weekend of our father's funeral, "Well, we survived." I had looked at him, wondering what he meant, but there was no time to talk. Why wasn't he coming to our mother's funeral? What was keeping him away?

I didn't want to be around when my sister and her husband arrived. I believed that all the anxiety my mother had experienced because of their behavior led to her heart attack. I didn't even want to go to the funeral. My daughter and I decided to stay overnight and leave in the morning.

I was worried about the journal that my mother had left on her nightstand: what she wrote about my sister and her husband and that when she died, she hoped "certain people" (she wouldn't go so far as to name names) wouldn't come to her funeral. I wondered whether to leave the journal, whether my sister should read it.

I woke up in the middle of the night. My mother hovered over my bed, a diaphanous ghost version of herself. She was trying to speak to me. I followed her into the hallway outside her bedroom. While her voice was garbled, I intuited that she was telling me that I should not let my sister see the journal.

The next morning my daughter and I started packing. We grabbed a few things: a couple "happy dolls" that my mother had made, a Victorian cranberry glass jar I had given her to add to her collection, several floral bone china teacups her sister Madge had given her, including her favorite violet floral one—and the journal by her bedside. Neighbors I had called with the news came by to offer their condolences. They asked if they could have something that she made, some remembrance. They were so pleased when I let them each pick out one of my mother's dolls.

My daughter and I went into town for a quick breakfast and then returned to the house to see if Doug was there yet. When I pulled my mother's car up to the curb, he came out to greet us but cautioned me not to go back into the house. My sister and her husband had arrived. I saw my brother-in-law Jim peering through the sheer curtains in the picture window. My daughter was leaning against the front of the car, holding her violin. Suddenly Jim opened the front door and walked toward us. "I couldn't," he stuttered. "Seeing your daughter standing there, it-it didn't seem right." He must have been wondering what she was thinking about all this craziness, wondering why she couldn't go into her beloved grandmother's house, wondering about family, whether this is what families are like.

"You're family," Jim said. "We'll go to the service together."

Jim signaled us to come into the house. That night he took us all out to dinner. He had a request. Would Angela play her violin at the service? Yes, she would. For her gran, she must have been thinking.

Cynthia and Jim and Doug and Nancy went back to the Holiday Inn and my daughter and I stayed at the house. I was so glad my daughter was there, her presence enabling some light to shine on the disturbing darkness.

There was hardly anyone at the funeral service. The neighbors stayed away. They later told me they were afraid my mother would be placed in an open casket and they couldn't bear to look at her. My daughter played a beautiful Bach sonata on her violin.

After the service, we went back to the house. While we were sitting around the dining room table, my sister said that she had opened a box of letters in the closet in the guest room and found a letter from Aunt Madge cautioning our mother about seeing some man where she worked as a bookkeeper in Springfield, Massachusetts. Shocked that she told what felt to me like such an inappropriate story, I got up from the table and went back into the closet and returned with a beautiful framed hand-tinted studio portrait (1932) of her/my/our! mother with her first-born child, my sister. My sister looked at the photograph as if she had never pictured such a relationship with her mother. Everyone at the table glowed with pleasure.

Later that day, my sister and her husband transferred the title of my mother's car to my daughter. We would drive it back home and she could use it in college. After my sister signed the form, she turned to me and said, "There, we've made up." I looked at her quizzically.

Back home four months later, while waiting in line for a college graduation ceremony to begin, I talked briefly about my sister to a colleague in the psychology department, who was also a family therapist. She told me that it was up to me to break the cycle of family dysfunction. I said that I had sent one of my mother's floral bone china teacups to my sister on her birthday, a month after our mother's death day, and she was pleased. "Try again—not on her birthday," the therapist said, as the line began to move, followed by, "Good luck with your sister."

rumors

A MONTH AFTER my mother died, Jerry arranged a small gathering at his house in East Longmeadow, Massachusetts, for a few relatives and friends who were unable to go to the funeral. Jerry wore a formal-looking navy blue suit and was seated at one end of a long, oval table, his wife at the other end. I sat on his right side next to Aunt Peggy. My daughter and her boyfriend sat across from me.

Aunt Peggy said that she had planned to visit my mother in April. Uncle Webb said that he had talked to her by phone the day before she died. I told the story of how when I went to take a photo of Aunt Peggy and my mother on their London visit, they discovered they were wearing the same style sweater but in different colors. My childhood friend Patty was fondly recalling my mother when suddenly Jerry interrupted.

"I don't have good memories," he said. Aunt Peggy looked up, shocked, her eyes directed at my brother like headlights at high beam. Jerry rubbed his finger on a reddish line between his eyebrows and said, "This is where the coat hanger got me."

The conversation came to an abrupt stop as if he had stood up and pulled out a handgun. My daughter and her boyfriend simultaneously rose and began clearing the table. "Is everyone done with dessert?" my daughter said.

I remember hearing when I was a child some reference to an abortion attempt by my mother when she was pregnant with Jerry. His wife later told me that Aunt Madge had told him about it, but my sister said that never happened. "That scar was from chicken pox," she scoffed. Aunt Madge I knew to be a reliable source, but why would she tell my brother? Years later, I asked Jerry's wife again. "He did not make that up," she said. We will never know the truth. What matters is that Jerry believed his mother tried to abort him. The story remains buried with my mother and my aunt—and my brother Jerry.

popsicle anyone?

MY BROTHER DOUG died an untimely death at age sixty-seven. He had stopped going on an annual fishing trip to Maine with his friends. He was too tired. By the time he questioned his doctor's diagnosis that asthma was slowing him down, making it hard for him to mow the lawn even, it was too late. Six months after his retirement party, he was dead from inhaling a chemical at the New England Door Closer, Inc. where he worked for forty years. He hadn't wanted to sue the company: "They no longer use the chemical. They didn't know at the time." And the doctor who had misdiagnosed his illness? "No malpractice suit," he told his wife.

When I went to visit Doug in the hospital, I heard laughter coming from his room as I walked down the hall. My brothers had bonded again. Jerry and Doug were telling stories. Doug smiled seeing me and said I looked good. "Is it true you two climbed a ladder at Wilson's Rest Home and peered into the windows and made scary faces and sounds, frightening the residents?"

They laughed.

"I love you, Pammy," Doug said.

His doctor came in with a pair of crutches; it was time for Doug to start walking.

Picture my brother on crutches trying to walk along the hospital corridor, his doctor coaching him, Doug wearing an earnest I-can-do-it-look: "If only I can do it, then . . ." He stopped. Then morphine. Popsicles for food. Family all around as if it were a Memorial Day picnic in the backyard.

His last sentence: "Popsicle anyone?"

HEALING FROM TRAUMA

healing from trauma

A Participant Observer's Report

"Maybe the body remembers what the mind wants to forget."

—Kate Zambreno

THE TURKEY DAY trauma that was stuck waited a long time—decades—and then started demanding I pay attention. IT wanted out. In 2002, I tried to dull the knot-like ache that sometimes settled in my stomach and other times in my heart (that's how it felt) by taking Lexapro, a drug my doctor in Upstate New York recommended. He said it would help balance serotonin levels in my brain and reduce anxiety. The drug toned down my feeling anxious but felt numbing like a mask that was covering something up. Deeper healing wasn't happening.

Also around this time, I started seeing a cognitive behavior therapist (CBT) who helped me explore repressed memories and feelings. She asked me to keep a journal. Here are two early entries:

HOWL

How did I get here in this hollow place
where the wind howls
and I look out
and see only dark,
which means I can't see,
I can't see anything.
I only hear wind howling,
forced air venting
breath of fire.
I am cold, cold as death.
You'll catch your death,
my mother used to say,
in that cold.

GRAY

I'm washed up.
Life is gray.
I'm washed out.

"Gray is the color of abandonment," my therapist said.

I did "inner child" work to help her (who was me) come to voice. As suggested, I used a photograph of myself as a little girl to write a Dear Pammy letter, assuring her she was safe now.

Dear Pammy,

It's safe to come out now. You don't have to hold yourself tight like your mother held you in her womb, in the amniotic sac where you lay waiting to enter the world, listening to sounds of discord that vibrated louder and louder, negatively charging the fluid where you lay submerged, your heart beating faster-faster, your body growing. You held back coming into the world as long as you could as if you feared exiting. At eight pounds you couldn't hold out any longer. You were healthy but had to wait two weeks to go home because your mother needed hospital care. And you needed a name, which your Aunt Madge gave you, not your mother, not your father.

You were put in a crib in the dining room where you lay staring at the flowered wallpaper. Joy was a streak of light coming through a window and shining on you. The light spoke to you: you felt the light.

You've developed a many-layered, thick coat of armor, and I see you've removed this shield now and feel vulnerable and understandably a little afraid to let go. But you are ready now. Put your feet on the ground Balance yourself. Walk freely. You can even smile at fear and let your inner light glow. Think of this time as a time of rebirth and bring the light that shines within you wherever you go, spreading the light. Have compassion for yourself and for all living beings.

Later in your life, your mother too-often-for-your-comfort called you "the good mistake" and you heard "mistake," but she always emphasized "good" as in a mistake that turned out to be "good." So "baby girl," as your mother also called you endearingly as a grown adult, go forth. Be here where you are now.

While talk therapy helped, something traumatic remained stuck.

I even tried scream therapy. After a kinesiologist I had also been seeing used muscle testing and acupressure to locate where in my body the trauma was stored (in my heart that day), he sent me downstairs into the basement and told me to scream loud and keep escalating. After the session, I grabbed a pencil and scribbled about my experience:

The Scream

Exhausted from suppressing the scream, lips quiver now as the scream rises, racing like hot lava through my veins. Cold sweat shivers skin. Limbs tremble tremor. The scream, urgent now, pushes, pulsating upward. Strength dissipates from years of holding the scream in. There's no fight left, no controlling the scream now. The scream, no longer buried, surges upward, outward, and erupts a whisper, breaking silence.

The trauma persisted. My stomach still felt tied in a knot. I decided to see the doctor who had put me on Lexapro, but he was not available, so I saw another doctor in the practice. "Maybe you have adrenal fatigue. I don't know what to do with you," she said to me bent over with pain. "Whether to send you to a gastroenterologist—or a therapist," she added as if exasperated. "I already see a therapist," I whimpered. She told me she'd be back, that she had to see another patient who was waiting. I managed to get up and leave.

When I went back to my own doctor who at least took time with me, he suggested I try Cymbalta, a new drug approved by the Food and Drug Administration in 2004 for the treatment of generalized anxiety disorder. After one month, however, the effects were negative to the point that I started feeling suicidal. I was going in the opposite direction of healing. I felt as if I were losing my mind. If I kept taking Cymbalta, I could end up being institutionalized like my father—or like women in the nineteenth century who were declared lunatics and sent off to asylums, often for the rest of their lives. I subsequently learned that this drug had only been tested for six months and many people were reporting suicidal thoughts as a "side effect."

While doing some research, I came across a book about eye movement desensitization and reprocessing (EMDR), a psychotherapy that enables people to heal from the symptoms and emotional distress that are the result of disturbing life experiences. Fortunately, the cognitive behavior therapist I was seeing knew a trauma therapist who was trained to do EMDR therapy. She had studied with Bessel van der Kolk, internationally acclaimed for his research on the effects of trauma on the mind and body, which he later wrote about in *The Body Keeps the Score: Brain, Mind, and Body in the Healing of Trauma* (2014). His primary argument is that to successfully treat psychological trauma we cannot discount the bodily symptoms of traumatized people. As our minds try to leave trauma behind, our bodies keep us trapped in the past. EMDR therapy releases the trapped trauma.

I was eager to try this treatment and, fortunately, was able to get an appointment right away. However, the trauma therapist could not start treating me until I had withdrawn completely from Cymbalta. She arranged for me to see a psychiatrist immediately. He would tell me how to decrease the dosage and what time frame I could expect. I would only have to go for one appointment. "You don't have to like him," she said as if to warn me.

I expected that I would be in and out of his office. I didn't expect him to ask me what a psychotherapist would ask: what's bothering you, what's on your mind, why did you start taking this drug? I sat in a chair against a wall opposite his desk across the room. I couldn't move or look at him. The drug had hold of me. I stared into space: an image of my father in a deranged mental state suddenly came to mind.

The psychiatrist was cold and removed. I couldn't speak to him. I felt as if I were under investigation. "Well, if you aren't going to speak to me, I can't help you," he said matter-of-factly. I needed him. I needed to get off this drug. "Perhaps you don't like me and you'd like to see someone else," he said, ready to dismiss me. Tears rolled down my cheeks as I somehow uttered a sentence about my father's shock treatment. Fortunately, he didn't inquire further and outlined a withdrawal plan and handed it to me.

I met weekly with the trauma therapist during the withdrawal period. She checked to see how I was doing and also asked about my history. I felt comfortable with her. She told me she would be acting as a guide rather than as an analyst. Insights would come from my exploring negative emotions caused by unresolved earlier traumatic experience. She explained that EMDR therapy uses rapid eye movement (REM) to help integrate the two sides of the brain so that I would recall a traumatic memory more like a story from the past than a reenactment in the present.

I'm going to bring in Bessel van der Kolk to explain briefly the differences in the two sides of our brains.

> The left brain remembers facts, statistics, and the vocabulary of events. We call on it to explain our experiences and put them in order. The right brain stores memories of sound, touch, smell and the emotions they evoke... Under ordinary circumstances the two sides of the brain work together... [However] when something reminds traumatized people of the past, their right brain reacts as if the traumatic event were happening in the present. But because their left

brain is not working very well, they may not be aware that they are re-experiencing and reenacting the past . . . The rational [left] brain is basically impotent to talk the emotional [right] brain out of its own reality. (44-47)

The therapist reminded me that the "R" in EMDR stands for "reprocessing," using REM to digest the trauma and store it appropriately in the brain. I will discard negative emotions, beliefs, and body sensations. If I witness something that triggers a traumatic memory, I will remember more like an observer. I was so ready to get started!

In an early session, I brought a booklet of some startling black-and-white images I had created years earlier using a photocopier. I had just trimmed my long hair and wondered how the cut would look photocopied. I used white paper as a mask to cover my face, pulled my hair around the edges, and pressed "Copy." I found the image intriguing. It captured the haircut on a faceless face. Where a face would be in a mirror or photograph there was white space. Feeling playful, I crinkled the paper, cut horizontal slits for eyes, and included my hand in some of the images to look as if it were making an adjustment.

I was startled by the disturbing images I had produced. It was if my body had found a way to get my attention. I spread them out on a table and selected ten to arrange in a series I called "Bodystory: Unmasking a Self," followed by this explanation: "I am using the mask to uncover a Self, a story, a dark story that runs beneath the Self: an untold story of buried pain that is trying to express itself."

"Choose an image that is most disturbing," the therapist said. I flipped through the booklet and pointed to this image.

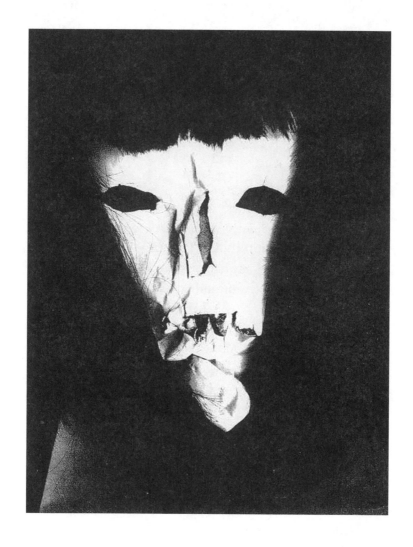

"Let's focus on that. On a scale of zero to ten, how disturbing is this image right now?"

"Ten," I said.

"How does it make you feel?"

"I feel scared."

"Where do you feel this emotion in your body?"

"My stomach feels tied in a knot."

"What's the positive belief you want to install?"

"I feel safe."

"On a scale of one to seven, ranging from 'doesn't feel true' to 'feels true,' what number would you pick now?"

"Definitely a one."

Then the therapist directed me to begin the bilateral stimulation of my brain. I had two choices. I could either focus my eyes on the moving hand of the therapist or hold two vibrating devices, one in each hand, that alternate right-left. I chose the latter because I could access my memories faster and more intensely. When I shut my eyes, the disturbing image immediately appeared. After a couple of minutes, the therapist stopped the vibrations and asked, "What's coming up?"

"My father being carried out in a straitjacket on a stretcher on Turkey Day, his eyes darting wildly back and forth."

"Go with that," the therapist said as she turned on the vibrators.

"What's coming up now?" she asked.

"Fear. *Will I lose my mind?*"

At the end of each session, which included several bilateral brain stimulations, the therapist asked me to scan my body to see if the number indicating stress was lower and the number for establishing a positive belief was higher. While fragments of the past began to knit together, the memory of my father's breakdown and shock treatment would take more time to process.

I went to see the movie *Eternal Sunshine of the Spotless Mind* (2004) about an estranged couple literally erasing each other from their memories through some kind of treatment. The idea seemed interesting, especially after a breakup. Unfortunately, I didn't read the rest of the synopsis to learn that the treatment was electroshock therapy.

When the movie showed the man with electrodes placed on his scalp and having what looked like a seizure, my body went into shock. I sat frozen in my seat. I had to struggle with my weighted-down body to leave the theater. It was indeed as if my body remembered.

My therapist told me that I'd had a flashback. Watching someone in a movie being treated with electroshock therapy triggered a traumatic memory of my father's experience that caused me to relive the event as if it were happening in the present. Again, she assured me that as I continued doing EMDR therapy, I would be able to recognize a trigger and would be more of an observer. And that is what eventually happened.

Late in her life my mother began making her dolls. I have a photograph of her sitting on her living room couch cradling one of them, surrounded by a couple dozen other dolls. One time she sent me a photo of a doll she was in the process of making. She had finished the doll's head. The yellowish-orange yarn hair was sewn in place. This doll wasn't like the others. Her startled blue eyes were wide open under short, over-plucked brows that gave her an always-surprised look. Her nose, embroidered red, was in the shape of a comma turned on its side. Lips, too, were embroidered red and indented into her face so her cheeks puffed out, creating a perpetual smile. But what really alarmed me was the pin with a ball at the end woven in and out (dead center) of her neck. It triggered the frightening black and white mask-like face with a gnarled neck that symbolized the trauma I experienced, an untold story of buried pain that was trying to express itself.

Next to the photo, my mother had written "Name?" I am sure she thought the photo and question fun as she was running out of names for her many dolls. For me, however, it recalled her being asked that same question in the hospital when I was born and her not having an answer. Her sister Madge named me, not my mother or my father. It was a double trigger. I was speechless. But I was not re-traumatized. I could recognize I was being triggered. I was not upset with my mother who had been through so much herself, and I knew that sewing brought her so much pleasure. I was able to pause and recompose myself.

"How about naming her Julia, your middle name?" I suggested.

"Yes," she said. "What a good idea."

EMDR therapy helped me release the feeling of being abandoned: left Standing on a Curb, everything gone gray. I could still remember, but the trauma was no longer stuck. I could tell this story now.

Recently when I was browsing the Internet, I came across an article on HuffPost (April 13, 2017) called "40 Features of Post Traumatic Stress Disorder of Abandonment" by Susan Anderson, psychotherapist, author, workshop leader, and founder of the Abandonment Recovery Movement. Her groundbreaking program, based on thirty years of research and clinical practice, helps people heal abandonment trauma. I am especially glad for her naming abandonment as a kind of PTSD, and I'm so glad she's here, helping people with abandonment trauma from childhood as well as adult losses and disconnections.

During a Master Class I took with writer Lydia Davis, I looked at an earlier version of "Turkey Day." Influenced by my new freedom following EMDR therapy and reading magical realism at the time, I wanted to free the turkey: I wanted it to leave the scene, walk away, but magical realism seemed an incongruent turn. What I did instead was to *imagine* freeing the trauma on that day:

> *I rise and go to the porch, put on my father's plaid wool shirt and heavy garden gloves, and go back to get the turkey. I carry the turkey in its roasting pan up the garden path to the chicken coop, now garden shed. I lift*

the turkey, skin still sticking to the pan, and lower it into a bucket. Stuffing oozes through the flap of skin my mother had sewn tight. I carry the turkey beyond the plot of land my father gardened to the edge of the woods. There, I bury it.

The following spring, I wrote this journal entry about an actual burial:

I did a home burial this morning in my wildflower garden. Bright and sunny outside. Dug a hole, burnt the scary mask image, and planted a rose bush over the ashes. My father was a vegetable gardener and roses were the one flower he liked to plant. So to plant a rose bush over the Turkey Day image seemed right.

PERCEPTION

*The lens each person looks through is uniquely personalized,
and at first seems to be the only way to see, to experience.*

—Jan Frazier

*The true story lies
among other stories
a mess of colours, like jumbled clothing
thrown off or away,
like hearts on marble, like syllables, like
butchers' discards . . .*

—Margaret Atwood

"what goes around comes around"

I GAVE MY mother a pink-flowered journal for writing down thoughts that she couldn't say about how she felt. On the opening page, she wrote, "God give me calm and confidence—and please, a twinkle in the eye." She called the book her "friend" and wrote what was most painful in Gregg shorthand, so nobody could read it.

In her early entries, she wrote about the challenges of living with my father the year or so before he went to a nursing home. Off medication, his irritability had returned and increased. He didn't talk much and was often cross with her. Whenever I visited, she'd always say, "Remember, your father is a good man."

Later entries are about the "terrible day" of my father's funeral, when she felt so mistreated by my sister and her husband and was deeply hurt:

January 1996
It is two months now, and I hope the memory of that terrible day never returns.

What was done to me, I cannot forgive. I wish I could put it behind me. I will keep busy. I feel lonely.

It was so cruel! If I only knew why I am being treated like this.

February 1996 (after my sister called her)
So what if I wasn't myself. How could I be? Suffering from stress and exhaustion. Ah, the things I wanted to say to her but couldn't.

"What goes around comes around," my mother wrote. I pondered what she meant. Maybe my mother felt that justice would eventually come 'round.

When my mother returned to her home in Florida after her London visit, she wrote about her heartache, which I think is the best way to describe what she was feeling:

June 1996
Don't they know how exhausted and confused I was during those years when Charles was so ill? Why couldn't they be quiet and caring? How could they say the things to me that they did? There's so much I could say to them, but it would make an argument.

August 1996
I am better. Cynthia calls me once in a while, tries to sound like she used to, but nothing will ever be the same again between us.

Her last journal entry was written in the form of a poem.

December 1996
*There is a burden I must face
until I reach a better place.
Some day somehow I will be free
and then at last I will be me.*

When I am dead and gone
and my ashes are laid to rest
know that I did my very best.

Do I think my mother did her very best? Yes, I do. I really do.

"once again, let me say, what goes around comes around"

WHEN MY MOTHER declared again in her journal, "What goes around comes around," she seemed to be reminding herself of her trust in the biblical "As ye sow, so shall ye reap." I thought about this proverb when my sister called me, weeping, eighteen years after the weekend of our father's funeral. Now there weren't two brothers between my sister and me—or parents. There were just the two of us, and she was in trouble, my sister.

A cop had called her from South Carolina a few days earlier to tell her that he had her husband in custody. He was lost and confused and cold. "He must have been trying to get back to Massachusetts where he was born," my sister said. "He has Alzheimer's disease and took off in the middle of the night." She had been trying to get the keys away from him, but he wouldn't cooperate. Their son went to get him the next morning and arranged for him to be admitted to a hospital.

Cynthia had called me on the pretense of asking me to pay back the six hundred dollars Jim had loaned me twenty-six years ago, when I needed help with a transition in my life. I told her of course I would send her the money and apologized for the lateness. She told me not to worry. What she wanted was to talk.

"I'm scared," my sister said, sobbing again. "I don't know what to do." She feared she would lose everything: their house, their savings.

I was moved to tears myself, listening to my sister in distress. "How long has this been going on?" I asked.

I was surprised when she said "Nine years. Since we moved to Florida." She told me that the last few years she had felt like a prisoner in her own home. Her husband had become "verbally abusive" is how she put it. She was exhausted. "I'm too old to go through all this. It was a nightmare living with him these last couple of years," she said, sobbing again.

I wondered if this was what it would take for her to understand what our mother had suffered. As we talked over the next few weeks, intermittently I would say, lowering my voice to a whisper, "That's what Mom went through," and she'd say, "Yeah." Not "yeah, yeah," dismissive like our father, but "yeah" as a tentative acknowledgement perhaps. In an a-ha! moment, I realized that she was living what had "come around." So my mother was right: "What goes around comes around." But would what "comes around" lead to remorse, understanding, or compassion?

postscript (january 2014)

For every story, there is another story that stands before it.
—Kim Chermin

IN ANOTHER TELEPHONE conversation, when I had the courage to bring up the weekend that our father had died, my sister said, "I don't remember." I gently said a couple of things to trigger her memory—her pacing and complaining to our mother that the urn was not included and telling me to keep away. "I don't remember," she repeated. She said she was so upset that she just wanted to leave as fast as she could.

What she remembered vividly was going to the nursing home to see our father and finding him alone on a gurney in a corridor. He was in a fetal position. She was horrified. "His eyes were closed and his tongue was hanging out," she said. "And our mother wasn't paying any attention to him. She asked for some pain medication. For *herself.*" Determined to get his attention, Cynthia whispered in his ear, "Daddy, your favorite buddy's here," and "his eyes went bright at the sight of Jim."

I thought about how I storied—and stored—the scene the next day when I came through the door to our mother's house with a bag of groceries. My sister had just arrived from St. Pete, where she and Jim had spent the night. She didn't even greet me. She was pacing, looking at some papers about the funeral arrangements my mother had made, seemingly upset about an urn not being included. I realize now that her anger was an expression of the pain she felt seeing our father placed on a gurney with no one looking after him and our mother's strange behavior. No wonder she wanted to leave as fast as she could.

Why didn't my mother tell me about any of this? She had told me about my father's response when he saw Jim, but she went on to talk about how much my father liked him, that he was like a son. She said nothing about her husband being left on a gurney, as if on his way to be black bagged. And when I said, "He won't last the night," she said, "Maybe there's something on TV," as if she hadn't heard me. She had fallen and sprained her ankle and couldn't go back to see him. She wanted me to get a movie. I wanted to be with my father. I didn't want him to die alone. Why was our mother acting like this? Maybe it was her way of coping with her grief. And thus the drinking, the pills. When I tried to talk with her about what was going on, she said she didn't know what I was talking about, her eyes glued to the TV screen.

I wish Cynthia could have taken me aside and shared with me what she had witnessed that afternoon, but she couldn't. I wish I had been able to call her when I was confused about our mother's behavior early during my stay. I would have liked some support. I dialed her number but hung up, afraid she'd be angry with me. I was also protective of my mother. I didn't want to say anything against her.

I remember how my sister had become more insistent about our mother moving into assisted living. Maybe she didn't know what else to do. She had her own problems: increased anxiety, high blood pressure, panic attacks. And her husband's business was in jeopardy.

I also learned that there was more to my sister's story, going further back. When my mother decided to move to Miami to be near my sister, I thought my parents flew together and that she was going to transfer him to a psychiatric hospital there. "No, no," my sister said. "That's not what happened."

What she told me surprised me. Our mother sent our father alone on a plane to Miami, while she packed up the house and prepared to sell it. My sister had three young children at the time; the oldest was six. When taking our father home from the airport, he tried to jump out of the car. My sister couldn't manage with him in the house. She couldn't leave him alone. When she found him wild-eyed in the bathroom trying to kill himself with a razor blade, she sent him back on a plane.

My sister also told me that our mother had complained to her about the boxes of books I sent ahead of my visit. "She played us off each other," she said.

I couldn't—or didn't want to—believe my mother would do that. I was "the good mistake."

postscript (february 2014)

I CALLED MY sister just before she was leaving Florida to go back to Long Island, where her husband was in a nursing home near their two daughters. I said something about how what she had been going through with him was like what our mother went through. She said she didn't know, that she had no idea. Our mother never said. When she and her husband took our parents on vacation, our father was always quiet and our mother complained and was mean to him. My sister did not consider that perhaps her behavior was a kind of release from the eerily cold silence she was living through after he stopped taking medication, a silence broken only by his snapping at her if she asked him to help with something or tried to have a conversation with him.

When I read my sister the poem our mother wrote about going to "a better place" where she could be herself, my sister wept. For a moment, it felt to me that we shared compassion for our mother, but my mother's voice lingered: *What was done to me I cannot forgive.* Then I remembered the therapist telling me that it was up to me to break the cycle of family dysfunction.

and the word was good

MY SISTER AND I started talking every couple of weeks. When I was finishing this manuscript, she called and I said, "I was just thinking of you."

"You were?" she said with a lilt in her voice.

"Yes."

"Was it good?"

"Yes, yes, it was good."

POSTLUDE

There's a crack, a crack in everything.
That's how the light gets in.

—Leonard Cohen

the way it is

There's a thread you follow. It goes among
things that change. But it doesn't change.
People wonder about what you are pursuing.
You have to explain about the thread.
But it is hard for others to see.
While you hold it you can't get lost.
Tragedies happen; people get hurt
or die; and you suffer and get old.
Nothing you do can stop time's unfolding.
You don't ever let go of the thread.

—William Stafford

backstory:

my mother's storage problem

MY MOTHER'S STORAGE problem started early—both her parents went missing. "Whatchya doin'?" relatives used to ask my mother when she was a child. "I'm seefin'," she'd say. "I was just seeing how things are, that's seefin'," she explained to me, a child sitting up in bed, home from school with chicken pox or measles. But it wasn't until I was much older that she told me about being called Honey Doola. That's how she said her name, Helen Julia, at age five, the year her mother died while trying to abort what would have been a seventh child.

Her father quickly remarried a woman called Charlotte, who went by Lottie. "Naughty Lottie" was a family legend. Naughty, as in mean and cruel. The story goes that she held my mother's face under the kitchen faucet and turned the water on cold until she turned blue in the face, what today would be called waterboarding. "Naughty Lottie" struck her twice, the second time with a brick she threw at my mother who was standing by a barn, and if she hadn't ducked . . . This wicked stepmother's behavior spoke loud and clear that she didn't want my mother around. Why not?

Because my mother looked like her mother, and Lottie didn't want to be reminded of her husband's late wife.

Abandoned by both parents, my mother was shuffled back and forth across the Vermont-Canadian border from one relative to another. She remembered hiding under a dining room table in Coaticook, Quebec, her old aunts lifting the tablecloth, trying to get her to come out. When she went to live with a cousin in Brandon, Vermont, she was afraid to go home after school. Would her cousin be there? And if there, would she hit her? No wonder she kept everything stored inside.

Once when I was visiting and we were having tea together in the dining room, she rose and picked up a framed faded black and white photograph of her mother, who was maybe eighteen or nineteen. She looked so innocent, her skin so smooth, her dark brown hair stylishly curled in a bun, her lips with a slight smile. "I would like to have known her," my mother said. "My father wasn't around much. She must have had a hard life," she said, getting up to put the photograph back on the shelf next to a photo of herself, age nineteen, neither of them knowing what difficulties lay ahead.

FLASHBACK:

A LETTER FROM MY MOTHER

May 5, 1983

This is some of my life story . . .

Once upon a time, fifty-one years ago, I married a man I thought was happy and full of fun. It turned out he wasn't, but he was a good, moral, faithful man. I hadn't been married six months when I realized I had made a mistake. What an awful way to feel—and I was pregnant! And so I made the best of it, always thinking I could change him, but I never have. I still try. The years have not taken away my sense of humor. I have made some mistakes. In my anger, I struck back, especially in my youth. I ranted and raved and threw things and pounded the iron in the cellar. I should have taken him to a psychiatrist, but I didn't know then. Frankly, he was rotten, nasty to me and as I said, I struck back. Also, I made my own little private life by creating things with what I had—and I had my children. Except for you, none of them went to your father to discuss anything. One day he said, "Why do they always come where you are?" and I said, "Because I listen." He made a lot of you and read Bunny Blue. We both played with you.

I never minded being poor. It was a challenge to see what I could make out of nothing. And sometimes I was mean, and I shouldn't have been.

He didn't mean to be so cross and irritable. I know that now, but I was young and unhappy. Then I got my first job and things were somewhat better. You were eleven. So, there was some improvement and then came the illness. I guess I don't have to tell you about that. How I got through it, I don't know. He was just about at death's door. I don't even know how he got through it.

Let me tell you, he came home from the hospital a different man. He was the way he should have been in the first place. Suddenly he was interested in my health and welfare. Years ago, if I were ill, he became very angry and told me not to tell him about it. (There are days when he reverts back irritable and unreasonable—today is one of those days.)

So time went on and things were better. People at work were kind to me and I needed that.

Lately things are not so good. I really think he should have stayed on the medicine. I try to make light of everything, but he is so cross. There is nothing I can do about it. It really doesn't matter anymore because I have things to do. I tire easily and rest a lot.

I find myself snapping back at him and must stop it. I slam doors and it makes me feel better. Frankly we don't talk too much because it seems I always say the wrong thing. I write some in my book.

When I have a pain attack, he is very good at those times, full of concern and sympathy.

I know that some of the illness still lingers.

Not long ago one evening we discussed the past. I told him frankly what he had been like and what it did to me. He said he was sorry and didn't remember most of it.

Why did it have to be this way? Life could have been so different. I have often wondered what life would have been like if your father hadn't had this problem. Sometimes I have imagined what it would have been like. Foolish of me, isn't it? But I can still dream. So the years go on and I make the best of things at hand. We have enough to live on, and I can buy most things I want. It really isn't bothering me too much anymore. Guess I have become mellow. It's a lifetime and interesting, eh?

So now at least you have some of the story. Don't feel sad or take it to heart. Your father is a good man, and I know now he would do anything for me. Whatever I have to put up with doesn't matter anymore. I shall always be happy, no matter what.

I will say one more thing. His mother, I am sure, knew the situation. I could tell by the way she looked at me and little kind things she would do.

I have never said these things to anyone else. Perhaps it will do me good to put it in writing.

Love, Mum

FLASHBACK:

A CONVERSATION WITH MY FATHER

My father is eighty-six years old and sitting in his reclining chair in the living room. He beckons me to sit on the footstool. He has a request.

"I would like you to write a script and make a movie about your mother," he says. "Her life story," he adds.

I want to please him, though this is not the kind of writing I do, nor in fact the kind that would sell to a movie audience today.

"I have made notes," he says. "There was a woman . . ."

I look at him. I know the plot. Her mother died when she was five. Her stepmother didn't want her around because she looked like her mother. She was shuffled back and forth between Quebec and Vermont . . . I can see how this is going. It is sounding like a series of vignettes from the 1948 film *I Remember Mama*.

"Dad, I'm not that kind of writer, I . . ."

But he doesn't listen. He grows irritable and impatient. "It would be a big hit. She had many obstacles to overcome," he says, handing me his notes.

He looks across the room at a gold-framed painting of Uncle Frank's farmhouse in Brandon, Vermont. "It was kind of Frank to take her in," he says, "but she lifted those heavy pails of milk . . ." He drifts for a moment, and then looks at me as if I didn't know: "She only had one set of clothes in high school, *which she washed every night.*" (I say this last part with him, silently of course, to be respectful.) "Still, she was the class valedictorian," he adds, though there were actually two tied for the honor. The other girl was chosen to give the valedictorian speech to the class, which I know disappointed my mother terribly, though she never said. She gave me the pin with which she was presented. I don't tell this backstory to my father, who is on a roll with his story.

"She worked in a bookstore, too," he says.

I think of the inscription in a book of poems her supervisor, who was also a writer, gave her in 1929:

To Helen Carr, whose efficient work and genial nature have lightened my labors in the reorganization of a difficult department. With kind thoughts and best wishes for Christmas and all the coming years.
                                                        —Bunyan

I think "how sweet" until I happen to leaf through the book and find a note written by my mother, dated 1983.

It's hard to believe that this man—was a "dirty old man." I worked for him when I was nineteen and had forgotten he was so poetic among other things!!

An excerpt from his poem "Memory,"

Where'er I go on life's uncharted sea
Or on its aimless billows roll
I only ask that there may come to me
Rest at last in death of the soul . . .

Leafing through the book, I found this piece more telling:

"Onward Christian Soldier"
 (Sing softly on feeling the urge)
 I'm so glad I'm single.
 I'm so glad I'm free.
 No sweet singing siren
 will ever capture me.
 (Harshly on having advances repulsed)
 I'm so glad I'm single.
 I'm so glad I'm free.
 No designing female
 can get her hooks in me.

"Don't forget to include that she's a wonderful cook," I hear my father saying. "And her sewing, so talented. Remember that beautiful jacket she made me? She made her own patterns out of newspaper. She worked hard, your mother, don't forget." He drifts, looking far away as if tuning into a big screen.

"I won't forget," I say. "Have you told her these things?"

"No, no," he says. "I want it to be a surprise."

"Yeah, yeah," I want to say, which is what my father said when he wanted to be dismissive, which was more and more often.

"Well, it's a story all right," I say, "but you have to let the story lie around, see what happens."

"What're you talking about?" he asks. "This *is* the story," he says, pointing to his notes.

I don't want to argue with my father. He never liked an argument.

"What a tragedy," he says, closing his eyes now, leaning back in his recliner.

"Yeah, yeah," I say.

"Are you mocking me?" he asks, opening his eyes.

"No, no," I say, my hand on his folded hands now.

"I wanted to surprise her," he says, nodding off to sleep.

pretty good for a mother

MY MOTHER WAS on her own journey by the time I arrived later in her life. After her death, I found a letter her brother George, who served in the navy, wrote to her on December 28, 1944, a little over a month before I was born. *Dear Little Sister,* he began, and then thanked her for sending him and his service buddies some of her homemade fruitcake for Christmas. (My mother's recipe still makes the rounds over the holidays.) She had apparently confided in him about being upset that she was "in a predicament" (is how she put it). He wrote back that she wasn't too old to have another child and shouldn't "condemn herself," skipping over whatever she might have written about her often difficult life with my father. He ended by asking her to forgive him for not realizing her "circumstances" and told her he hoped along with her that she would have a girl.

During my childhood, my mother was worn down by my father's sometimes irritable behavior, but I surmise that she had come to accept her life by the time I came along. If she got upset, she did not confront him as she apparently did when my older siblings were around. She carried on as best she could. Her love of life always surpassed any difficulties.

Unlike my father, who was restrained by a straitjacket, she was restrained by circumstances. She continued to cook and host Sunday dinners and also my father's penny poker friends who occasionally gathered at our house. Picture her opening the cigar smoke-filled dining room with her homemade apple pies and the men oohing and aahing, always appreciative.

I remember an eerily quiet house. Picture me as a child looking through the dining room window at my mother bent over her flower garden, tossing weeds over her shoulder, or me Standing in the Hallway by the cellar door at the top of the stairs, hearing her pounding the iron on my father's starched shirts. Picasso's "Woman Ironing" comes to mind: a woman with hollowed eyes and sunken cheeks pressing down on an iron with all her will.

The only book in our house was *A Tree Grows in Brooklyn* (1943) by Betty Smith, a classic coming-of-age story that stood alone on a shelf. Here's one quote from the book: "Who wants to die? Everything struggles to live. Look at that tree growing up there out of that grating. It gets no sun, and water only when it rains. It's growing out of sour earth. And it's strong because its hard struggle to live is making it strong." Like that tree, my mother did the best she could "under the circumstances," which was pretty good for a mother.

I considered titling my memoir *Pretty Good for a Mother* but then there's Turkey Day. I never asked my mother what that day was like for her. What was *she* thinking when she paused in the kitchen doorway and turned around to ask me to watch the turkey? Why didn't she walk over and turn off the oven, make a phone call, and send me somewhere else? Why did she leave me alone?

I wasn't the only one in shock. She was in shock. She wasn't able to mother me. Then she fled, which is how it felt to me, and "fled" is how it must have felt to her. Desperate to get away, she headed for Florida, this time to stay, hoping a "change of scenery" would do her good.

To say that my mother did the best she could "under the circumstances" that life presented is true, but it marginalizes my own feelings of abandonment at age eighteen. Looking back, I realize that part of the reason—maybe *the* reason—for my quest to reconnect with my mother when my father was dying was the abandonment I'd felt as a young adult. I wanted the mother of my childhood—that mother, not the non-present mother of the Turkey Day trauma that felt like a family funeral: death of a family followed by a sudden shutdown, everything gone gray like a digital screen after a power surge.

grief, renewal, and hope

The past is so hard to shift. It comes with us like a chaperone, standing between us and the newness of the present—the new chance.

—Jeanette Winterson

WHILE THE WOUNDS we carry from growing up in fractured families stay with us, they do not have to control us. We don't have to go round and round over old ground. Grief can turn to sorrow, despair, misery. "Enough misery memoirs," I smile and say. How to move toward forgiveness—to have a heart so open with longing it overrides pain? "If home is an affliction, never fixed, never finished, then it is the reaching toward home, toward a connection, that is the cure," writes memoirist Harrison Candelaria Fletcher.

"I'm so glad you're here," my mother's voice echoes. But what can I do now? Look back at the past with forgiveness and compassion, including self-compassion. Here where I am writing, I pause and look up at the skylight and see a gray sky, but I trust now that above the clouds the sky is blue and spacious, like my inner space that is always there no matter what the weather. I end with hope: a place of possibility. *That's how the light gets in.*

"The snow was up to the mailbox when you were born," my mother liked to brag, followed by "You smiled everywhere we went." All my years growing up, I remained attached to my mother, the umbilical cord turned to an invisible golden thread that made it possible for me to survive and eventually to thrive.

It's my birthday, Groundhog Day—winter weather advisory, traveling hazardous, dinner celebration plans disabled, "snow up to the mailbox." I go for a walk outside the townhouse tucked in a wooded hillside where I live now, knowing that I will see my shadow and go back inside until the weather turns, the sun shines, and it's time to plant again.

> *[Y]our life is a thread, a narrative unspooling in time, and a story is a thread, but each of us is an island from which countless threads extend into the world. I have pulled out one thread from the tangle or tapestry of [a] particular time, and nothing in my account is untrue, except perhaps the coherence of a story when really there were many stories.*
>
> —Rebecca Solnit

endnotes

Rebecca Solnit, *The Faraway Nearby* (New York: Viking Press, 2013).

Robin Hemley, "Finding Your Form," *Turning Your Life into Fiction* (Cincinnati, OH: Story Press, 1994): 41.

PRELUDE

Turkey Day
An earlier version of "Turkey Day" was published in the *Paterson Literary Review* 30, (Spring 2001): 60-65.

The straitjacket was introduced in the late eighteenth century as a "humane" alternative to the iron collars and chains that had previously been used to restrain the mentally ill.

Shock Treatment
Northampton State Hospital, formerly called Northampton Lunatic Asylum, was built in 1856 and received its first patients in 1858.

Much has been written about the horrific conditions and practices of this institution that eventually closed and was demolished in 2006. (See www.northamptonstatehospital.org or scua.library. umass.edu/umarmot/northampton-state-hospital for more.)

Bessel van der Kolk. *The Body Keeps the Score: Brain, Mind, and Body in the Healing of Trauma* (New York: Penguin, 2014): 28.

See also J. Michael Moore and Anna Schuleit Haber, *Images of America: Northampton State Hospital* (Charleston, SC: Arcadia Publishing, 2014). Visual artist Anna Schuleit Haber created the sound installation *Habeas Corpus*, in which the abandoned architecture was turned into an instrument in a single performance of J. S. Bach's *Magnificat*. Unfortunately, I did not learn about the installation until too late. However, I did correspond with Anna Schuleit Haber; she tried to find my father's hospital records but was unsuccessful.

Note: My father was experiencing psychotic episodes but had been misdiagnosed as a paranoid schizophrenic. For a fuller discussion about dealing with the complexities of mental illness and schizophrenia in particular, see Esme Weijun Wang's *The Collected Schizophrenias* (Minneapolis, MN: Graywolf Press, 2019).

Jonathan Sadowsky, in his book *Electeroconvulsive Therapy in America* (Abingdon-on-Thames, UK, Routledge, 2017), traces the American history of one of the most controversial procedures in medicine.

Jonathan Sadowsky, "Electroconvulsive therapy: a history of controversy, but also of help," *The Conversation*, January 12, 2017, www.theconversation.com/electroconvulsive-therapy-a-history-of-controversy-but-also-of-help-70938.

Peter Haddad, Robert Kirk, and Richard Green. "Chlor-promazine, the First Antipsychotic Medication: History, Controversy and Legacy," *British Association for Psychopharmacology*, October 31, 2016, www.bap.org.uk/articles/chlorpromazine-the-first-antipsychotic.

Wesley Sheffield, "The Community Mental Health Act of 1963," *Young Minds Advocacy Project*, www.ymadvocacy.org/the-community-mental-health-act-of-1963.

A Change of Scenery

Robert Frost, "Home Burial," *Selected Poems of Robert Frost* (New York: Holt, Rinehart & Winston, 1963). Frost's dramatic poem "Home Burial" was written in 1914. He died in 1963, the year my father had his "nervous breakdown" and was hospitalized at Northampton State Hospital.

DECADES LATER: 1995

I'm So Glad You're Here

Carolyn Steedman, *Landscape for a Good Woman: A Story of Two Lives* (New Brunswick, NJ: Rutgers University Press, 1987): 122.

Welcome to Sun Ray Homes

John McPhee, *Oranges* (New York: Farrar, Straus and Giroux, 1966): 46.

Benjamin Rosenbaum, "The Orange," *Flash Fiction Forward* (New York: W. W. Norton, 2006): 135-137.

The lengthening of hemlines is a sign of a declining economy, according to the Hemline Index (established in 1926 by George Taylor, who noticed a connection between good times and short skirts).

My father was hired by Carlisle's Hardware in Springfield, Massachusetts, where he worked for forty years (1923–1963). He was a "nails, bolts, and screws" man who worked his way up to become manager of the tool department. The head of the company, F.E. Carlisle, who was considered a "progressive merchant," sent my father to national sales meetings and to various cities to learn more. He soon became well known in the hardware business nationally and was featured in *Hardware Age*, a leading trade magazine in the 1950s. However, Carlisle, always on the lookout to modernize, eventually decided to move sporting goods to the front of the store and tools to the rear and to replace my father with a younger man. My father later told me that earlier in his career, he had a chance for a better position in Chicago, but he turned it down because, as he put it, he was "loyal to the Carlisle family"—a decision he later regretted.

Reading Sharon Olds's poem "I Go Back to 1933" influenced me to look back at a "before" photo of my parents. In the next-to-last paragraph in this scene, I borrowed Olds's words: "Stop, don't do it."

Zip-A-Dee-Doo-Dah, Zip-A-Dee-Ay . . .
Mimi Schwartz. A comment on an earlier manuscript.

Days of Our Lives
Patricia Hampl, *I Could Tell You Stories* (NY: W. W. Norton, 1999).

Flounder Florentine
New Recipes from Moosewood Restaurant (Ithaca, NY: The Moosewood Collective, 1987): 174.

Heartache
Pema Chodron, *Living Beautifully* (Boulder, CO: Shambhala Publications, 2012).

HEALING FROM TRAUMA

Kate Zambreno, *Book of Mutter* (Cambridge, MA, MIT Press, 2017): 164.

Dr. Jeff Egler describes adrenal fatigue as "a phenomenon characterized by a disruption of your adrenal glands' ability to make cortisol in the right amounts at the right times in response to stress" (www.parsleyhealth.com/blog/video/3-ways-support-adrenals).

A study by Kathleen Kendall-Tackett shows how trauma produces the hormones epinephrine and cortisol, which dramatically affects the body's blood sugar, among myriad other functions.

Kathleen Kendall-Tackett, "Psychological Trauma and Physical Health," *Psychological Trauma: Theory, Research, Practice, and Policy*, American Psychological Association, 2009, Vol. 1, No. 1, 35-48.

I also learned that some doctors could spend more time with patients because they got perks from the pharmaceutical industry and/or got paid for prescribing certain drugs.

Francine Shapiro, *EMDR: Eye Movement Desensitization and Reprocessing* (New York: The Guilford Press, 2001). A 3rd edition was published by Guilford Press in 2018. Shapiro was an American psychologist and educator who originated and developed EMDR. She died June 16, 2019.

"What is EMDR?" EMDR Institute, www.emdr.com/what-is-emdr.

Bessel van der Kolk, *The Body Keeps the Score: Brain, Mind, and Body in the Healing of Trauma* (New York: Penguin Press, 2014): 44–47. This book was a *New York Times* best seller in 2019 and 2020.

Nelia Viveiros, "Review of 'The Body Keeps the Score: Brain, Mind, and Body in the Healing of Trauma' by Bessel van der Kolk." *Journal of Loss and Trauma* 22, no. 2 (2017): 167-169.

Susan Anderson, "40 Features of Abandonment," *HuffPost,* April 13, 2017, www.huffingtonpost.com/entry/40-features-of-post-traumatic-stress-disorder-of-abandonment_us_58ed2e74e-4b0145a227cb909.

PERCEPTION

Jan Frazier, *The Great Sweetening: Life After Thought*, 2017, www.ebookit.com.

Margaret Atwood, *True Stories* (New York: Simon & Schuster, 1981): 11.

Postscript (January 2014)
Kim Chermin, *In My Mother's House: A Memoir* (San Francisco, CA: MacAdam/Cage, 2003).

POSTLUDE

Leonard Cohen, "Anthem," *The Future*, Columbia: 1992: "There's a crack, a crack in everything. That's how the light gets in."

William Stafford, "The Way It Is," *Ask Me: 100 Essential Poems.* Copyright © 1977, 2014 by William Stafford and the Estate of

William Stafford. Reprinted with the permission of The Permissions Company LLC on behalf of Graywolf Press, Minneapolis, Minnesota, www.graywolfpress.org.

Flashback: A Letter from My Mother
My mother was seventy-four when she wrote this letter, my father eighty-one. I was thirty-eight.

Elaine Gilliam, *Family Skeletons – A Web of Mental Illness,* (Conshohocken, PA: Infinity Publishing, 2016). Gilliam writes about the mental illness that was rampant in the Gay family. Her mother was Ruth Gay, my father's sister, who had severe bipolar disorder.

Flashback: A Conversation with My Father
Our conversation took place in 1988, when my father was eighty-six. My mother was seventy-nine. I was forty-three. This flash memoir was inspired by "A Conversation with My Father" by Grace Paley.

Grief, Renewal, and Hope
Jeanette Winterson, *Why Be Happy When You Could Be Normal* (New York: Knopf, 2011).

Words by Harrison Candelaria Fletcher, tweeted by Dinty W. Moore (@brevitymag) on November 15, 2018.

Rebecca Solnit, "Your Life is a Thread," *The Faraway Nearby* (New York: Viking Press, 2013).

acknowledgments

I am grateful to the late Margaux Fragoso, author of the haunting memoir *Tiger, Tiger* (New York: Farrar, Straus and Giroux, 2011), for her insightful reading and repeatedly encouraging me to go back and work on this manuscript.

Thanks to editor CoCo Harris who published an earlier, shorter version of the story about the weekend of my father's funeral called "The Family Funeral" in *So Long: Short Memoirs of Loss and Remembrance* (Telling Our Stories Press, 2012). This version served to get me started on a journey of looking and looking again.

Thanks to Mimi Schwartz, who read an early draft of the story "I'm So Glad You're Here," which I wrote in third person. She was encouraging but told me that writing in first person would open up the story. And she was so right.

Thanks also to writer/editor Mindy Lewis whom Mimi Schwartz recommended for reading a later version of my manuscript. I especially appreciated the good questions she asked at that stage.

Thanks to Susan Brown, in a workshop in San Miguel de Allende, Mexico, for calling my story a quest and her insight that the real family funeral was back in 1963.

And thanks to Gordon Pradl for his careful reading of "Turkey Day" and his encouragement and support, going way back to my graduate study at New York University when he was my dissertation advisor—and that turkey was still stuck.

I am so grateful to my dear *reader extraordinaire* Mary Rose Webster for her insights and editing and reminding me that *voice* is central to memoir. She truly befriended my writing. And what fun we had talking about words during the last round of revision—and commas, and semi-colons, and colons.

I am also thankful for my yogi-friend Karen Catalano's support on this journey and her empathic reading and conversations.

Special thanks to my healing team, especially trauma therapist Kathleen DiFulvio-Kaepplinger.

And to my sister Cynthia for calling me when she was in trouble and for our reconnection for which I am "so glad."

I also want to express my gratitude to all the writers whose voices and spirit influenced me and helped me "come to voice."

Finally, thanks to the supportive team at She Writes Press. Special thanks to Brooke Warner for her vision, spirited leadership, and guidance; and to editorial project managers Cait Levin, who helped me at the start, and Shannon Green, for her patience and meticulous attention to detail. Also thanks to copyeditor Jennifer Caven and proofreaders Laura Matthews and Megan Hannum; Barrett Briske, for assistance preparing material for publicists and obtaining permission to use William Stafford's poem; graphic artist Julie Metz for her creative cover design based on a photograph I took of the sign; Ben Perini for the illustration; and interior designer Tabitha Lahr for her oh-so-fine formatting of my book!

Some flash memoir included in this book appeared originally in slightly different form in the following publications:

"Turkey Day," *Paterson Literary Review*
"A Conversation with My Father," *Brevity*

about the author

Photo © Chuck Haupt

PAMELA GAY is the recipient of a New York Foundation for the Arts (NYFA) award in creative nonfiction and an Independent e-Book Award for her memoir *Homecoming,* which combined text, image, and sound. An installation sponsored by the New York State Council on the Arts (NYSCA) included artifacts. Her writing has been published in *Brevity, Iowa Review, Midway Journal, Paterson Literary Review, Monkeybicycle, Grey Sparrow, Vestal Review,* and other literary journals, as well as in two anthologies. Gay is professor emerita at Binghamton University, State University of New York, where she taught courses in flash memoir and flash fiction. She lives in Upstate New York.

Website: pamela-gay.com

SELECTED TITLES FROM SHE WRITES PRESS

She Writes Press is an independent publishing company founded to serve women writers everywhere. Visit us at www.shewritespress.com.

Rethinking Possible: A Memoir of Resilience by Rebecca Faye Smith Galli. $16.95, 978-1-63152-220-8. After her brother's devastatingly young death tears her world apart, Becky Galli embarks upon a quest to recreate the sense of family she's lost—and learns about healing and the transformational power of love over loss along the way.

The Coconut Latitudes: Secrets, Storms, and Survival in the Caribbean by Rita Gardner. $16.95, 978-1-63152-901-6. A haunting, lyrical memoir about a dysfunctional family's experiences in a reality far from the envisioned Eden—and the terrible cost of keeping secrets.

Raising Myself: A Memoir of Neglect, Shame, and Growing Up Too Soon by Beverly Engel. $16.95, 978-1-63152-367-0. A powerfully inspiring and unflinchingly honest story of how best-selling author and abuse recovery expert Beverly Engel made her way in the world—in spite of her mother's neglect and constant criticism, undergoing sexual abuse at nine, and being raped at twelve.

Baffled by Love: Stories of the Lasting Impact of Childhood Trauma Inflicted by Loved Ones by Laurie Kahn. $16.95, 978-163152-226-0. For three decades, Laurie Kahn has treated clients who were abused as children—people who were injured by someone who professed to love them. Here, she shares stories from her own rocky childhood along with those of her clients, weaving a textured tale of the all-too-human search for the "good kind of love."

Painting Life: My Creative Journey Through Trauma by Carol K. Walsh. $16.95, 978-1-63152-099-0. Carol Walsh was a psychotherapist working with traumatized clients when she encountered her own traumatic experience; this is the story of how she used creativity and artistic expression to heal, recreate her life, and ultimately thrive.